the gospel of mark

MEN AS TREES, WALKING ...

inter-varsity press

He looked up and said,

'I see men as trees, walking . . .'

(Mark 8:24, KJV)

Mark's good news

You are about to read one of the most influential books the world has ever seen. It is not simply history or biography, though it contains elements of both. It is *gospel*, the Good News about Jesus.

Jesus never wrote a book, never commanded an army, never ruled a nation, yet his birth split time in two, and his life and death have had an incalculable influence on the last two thousand years in every continent and amongst every type of person. His life and death were like a mighty volcano that threw up not only a new community, the church, but a new kind of literature, the Gospels. There are four of them, four angles on Jesus, so to speak. They had no precursors and no authentic successors. They are all about this amazing person Jesus. And Mark, the companion and interpreter of the apostle Peter, wrote the first of them. Every short paragraph, every climactic saying or action in this fast-moving account prompts the question 'Who is this Jesus?' The hinge on which the whole account moves is Jesus' question: 'But who do you say I am?' and Peter's response: 'You are the Messiah.' That means, 'You are God's anointed rescuer for humankind, God's ultimate king.' (See Mark 8:29.)

That is how his contemporaries saw him. Over the centuries, however, it has been fashionable to dilute Jesus, to squeeze him into the fashionable contemporary worldview, so as to rob him of his immediacy and uncomfortable challenge. He is the 'gentle Jesus meek and mild' of the nursery, whose teaching on the brotherhood of man and the fatherhood of God is so bland that it is a wonder anyone wanted to crucify him. Some have seen him as the 'witty rabbi', 'the radical political leader', the 'wandering philosopher'. You may have come across some of the modern attempts to press Jesus into a predetermined mould. For A. N. Wilson, Jesus was a Jewish holy man who taught an inner morality, opposed the anti-Roman Jewish nationalism of his day – and paid the price. James, his brother, assured his followers that his death was all 'according to the scriptures'. Wilson, however, believes that Jesus stayed dead. Due to family likeness and general confusion James got mistaken for Jesus, and the idea spread that Jesus had been raised from the dead. Meanwhile Paul invented Christianity as history knows it! The distinguished New Testament scholar Dr Tom Wright looks at various reconstructions like this in his recent book, *Who Was Jesus?* He has no difficulty in showing that they all rest on unrestrained imagination and an incurable preference for inferior evidence. You will not find any of either in Mark's terse compelling account.

Read Mark's Gospel for yourself and see if it does not have a ring of truth about it. Then make up your own mind. Whatever you decide, you will have done the honest thing. You will have consulted the 'primary source' rather than the 'literature on the subject'. You will have rubbed shoulders with a man whose home was the headquarters for the new Christian movement in Jerusalem: in all probability the Last Supper took place in his house. You will have reflected on the unadorned, non-chronological account of Jesus given by the man who assisted the two greatest missionaries, Peter and Paul, in evangelizing a good deal of the known world within a generation of the death and resurrection of Jesus.

The Christian faith differs from all others in a variety of ways, but in none more than this: it depends entirely on the identity of its founder. Confucianism, Buddhism and Hinduism would stand whether or not their founders ever lived: it is the teaching which matters. Not so with the Jesus who claims to be the bridge between God and man, a bridge securely fastened on both sides of the gulf. Once blow up that bridge and you will have destroyed Christianity. Nobody has managed it yet. But examine this Gospel, this firsthand evidence about Jesus, for yourself. Read it thoughtfully. And as you immerse yourself in the story, begin to frame a reply to Jesus' seminal question on which the whole Gospel hangs: 'Who do you say that I am?'

the Gospel of Mark

the message of John the Baptist

the preaching of John the Baptist

1 This is the good news about Jesus Christ, the Son of God. 1
2 It began just as God had said in the book written by Isaiah
the prophet,

> 'I am sending my messenger
>   to get the way ready for you.
> 3 In the desert someone is shouting,
> "Get the road ready for the Lord!
>   Make a straight path for him." '

4 So John the Baptist appeared in the desert and told
everyone, 'Turn back to God and be baptized! Then your sins
will be forgiven.'
5 From all Judea and Jerusalem crowds of people went to
John. They told how sorry they were for their sins, and he baptized them in the River Jordan.
6 John wore clothes made of camel's hair. He had a
leather strap around his waist and ate grasshoppers and wild
honey.
7 John also told the people, 'Someone more powerful is
going to come. And I am not good enough even to stoop down

1:7 untie his sandals: *this was the duty of the slave*

and untie his sandals. 8I baptize you with water, but he will baptize you with the Holy Spirit!'

The baptism and temptation of Jesus

the baptism of Jesus

9About that time Jesus came from Nazareth in Galilee, and
John baptized him in the River Jordan. 10As soon as Jesus
came out of the water, he saw the sky open and the Holy
Spirit coming down to him like a dove. 11A voice from heaven
said, 'You are my own dear Son, and I am pleased with you.'

Jesus and Satan

12Straight away God's Spirit made Jesus go into the desert.
13He stayed there for forty days while Satan tested him.
Jesus was with the wild animals, but angels took care of him.

Jesus in Galilee

Jesus begins his work

14After John was arrested, Jesus went to Galilee and told the
good news that comes from God. 15He said, 'The time has
come! God's kingdom will soon be here. Turn back to God and
believe the good news!'

Jesus chooses four fishermen

16As Jesus was walking along the shore of Lake Galilee, he
saw Simon and his brother Andrew. They were fishermen and
were casting their nets into the lake. 17Jesus said to them,
'Come with me! I will teach you how to bring in people instead

of fish.' 18At once the two brothers dropped their nets and went with him.

19Jesus walked on and soon saw James and John, the sons of Zebedee. They were in a boat, mending their nets. 20At once Jesus asked them to come with him. They left their father in the boat with the hired workers and went with him.

a man with an evil spirit

21Jesus and his disciples went to the town of Capernaum. Then on the next Sabbath he went into the Jewish meeting place and started teaching. 22Everyone was amazed at his teaching. He taught with authority, and not like the teachers of the Law of Moses. 23Suddenly a man with an evil spirit in him entered the meeting place and yelled, 24'Jesus from Nazareth, what do you want with us? Have you come to destroy us? I know who you are! You are God's Holy One.'

25Jesus told the evil spirit, 'Be quiet and come out of the man!' 26The spirit shook him. Then it gave a loud shout and left.

27Everyone was completely surprised and kept saying to each other, 'What is this? It must be some new kind of powerful teaching! Even the evil spirits obey him.' 28News about Jesus quickly spread all over Galilee.

Jesus heals many people

29As soon as Jesus left the meeting place with James and John, they went home with Simon and Andrew. 30When they got there, Jesus was told that Simon's mother-in-law was sick in bed with fever. 31Jesus went to her. He took hold of her hand and helped her up. The fever left her, and she served them a meal.

32That evening after sunset, all who were sick or had

1:32 after sunset: *The Sabbath was over, and a new day began at sunset.*

demons in them were brought to Jesus. [33]In fact, the whole town gathered around the door of the house. [34]Jesus healed all kinds of terrible diseases and forced out a lot of demons. But the demons knew who he was, and he did not let them speak.

[35]Very early the next morning, Jesus got up and went to a place where he could be alone and pray. [36]Simon and the others started looking for him. [37]And when they found him, they said, 'Everyone is looking for you!'

[38]Jesus replied, 'We must go to the nearby towns, so that I can tell the good news to those people. This is why I have come.' [39]Then Jesus went to Jewish meeting places everywhere in Galilee, where he preached and forced out demons.

Jesus heals a man

[40]A man with leprosy came to Jesus and knelt down. He begged, 'You have the power to make me well, if only you wanted to.'

[41]Jesus felt sorry for the man. So he put his hand on him and said, 'I want to! Now you are well.' [42]At once the man's leprosy disappeared, and he was well.

[43]After Jesus strictly warned the man, he sent him on his way. [44]He said, 'Don't tell anyone about this. Just go and show the priest that you are well. Then take a gift to the temple as Moses commanded, and everyone will know that you have been healed.'

[45]The man talked about it so much and told so many people, that Jesus could no longer go openly into a town. He had to stay away from the towns, but people still came to him from everywhere.

1:40 leprosy: *In biblical times the word 'leprosy' was used for many different kinds of skin diseases.*

1:44 everyone will know that you have been healed: *People with leprosy had to be examined by a priest and told that they were well (that is, 'clean') before they could once again live a normal life in the Jewish community. The gift that Moses commanded was the sacrifice of some lambs together with flour mixed with olive oil.*

Jesus heals a crippled man

2

Jesus went back to Capernaum, and a few days later
people heard that he was at home. 2Then so many of
them came to the house that there wasn't even standing room left in front of the door.

Jesus was still teaching 3when four people came up, carrying a crippled man on a mat. 4But because of the crowd,
they could not get him to Jesus. So they made a hole in the
roof above him and let the man down in front of everyone.

5When Jesus saw how much faith they had, he said to the
crippled man, 'My friend, your sins are forgiven.'

6Some of the teachers of the Law of Moses were sitting
there. They started wondering, 7'Why would he say such a
thing? He must think he is God! Only God can forgive sins.'

8Straight away, Jesus knew what they were thinking, and
he said, 'Why are you thinking such things? 9Is it easier for
me to tell this crippled man that his sins are forgiven or to tell
him to get up and pick up his mat and go on home? 10I will
show you that the Son of Man has the right to forgive sins
here on earth.' So Jesus said to the man, 11'Get up! Pick up
your mat and go on home.'

12The man got straight up. He picked up his mat and went
out while everyone watched in amazement. They praised God
and said, 'We have never seen anything like this!'

Jesus chooses Levi

13Once again, Jesus went to the shore of Lake Galilee. A
large crowd gathered around him, and he taught them. 14As
he walked along, he saw Levi, the son of Alphaeus. Levi was
sitting at the place for paying taxes, and Jesus said to him,
'Come with me!' So he got up and went with Jesus.

2:4 roof: *In Palestine the houses usually had a flat roof. Stairs on the outside led up to the roof that was made of beams and boards covered with packed earth.*

[15]Later, Jesus and his disciples were having dinner at Levi's house. Many tax collectors and other sinners had become followers of Jesus, and they were also guests at the dinner.

[16]Some of the teachers of the Law of Moses were Pharisees, and they saw that Jesus was eating with sinners and tax collectors. So they asked his disciples, 'Why does he eat with tax collectors and sinners?'

[17]Jesus heard them and answered, 'Healthy people don't need a doctor, but sick people do. I didn't come to invite good people to be my followers. I came to invite sinners.'

people ask about going without eating

[18]The followers of John the Baptist and the Pharisees often went without eating. Some people came and asked Jesus, 'Why do the followers of John and those of the Pharisees often go without eating, while your disciples never do?'

[19]Jesus answered:

The friends of a bridegroom don't go without eating while he is still with them. [20]But the time will come when he will be taken from them. Then they will go without eating.

[21]No one patches old clothes by sewing on a piece of new cloth. The new piece would shrink and tear a bigger hole.

[22]No one pours new wine into old wineskins. The wine would swell and burst the old skins. Then the wine would

2:15 tax collectors: *These were usually Jewish people who paid the Romans for the right to collect taxes. They were hated by other Jews who thought of them as traitors to their country and to their religion.*

2:18 without eating: *The Jewish people sometimes went without eating (also called 'fasting') to show their love for God or to show sorrow for their sins.*

2:22 swell and burst the old skins: *While the juice from grapes was becoming wine, it would swell and stretch the skins in which it had been stored. If the skins were old and stiff, they would burst.*

be lost, and the skins would be ruined. New wine must be
put into new wineskins.

a question about the Sabbath

23One Sabbath Jesus and his disciples were walking through
some wheat fields. His disciples were picking grains of wheat
as they went along. 24Some Pharisees asked Jesus, 'Why are
your disciples picking grain on the Sabbath? They are not supposed to do that!'

25Jesus answered, 'Haven't you read what David did when
he and his followers were hungry and in need? 26It was during the time of Abiathar the high priest. David went into the
house of God and ate the sacred loaves of bread that only
priests are allowed to eat. He also gave some to his followers.'

27Jesus finished by saying, 'People were not made for the
good of the Sabbath. The Sabbath was made for the good of
people. 28So the Son of Man is Lord over the Sabbath.'

a man with a crippled hand

3

The next time that Jesus went into the meeting place,
a man with a crippled hand was there. 2The
Pharisees wanted to accuse Jesus of doing something wrong, and they kept watching to see if Jesus would
heal him on the Sabbath.

3Jesus told the man to stand up where everyone could see
him. 4Then he asked, 'On the Sabbath should we do good
deeds or evil deeds? Should we save someone's life or
destroy it?' But no one said a word.

5Jesus was angry as he looked around at the people. Yet
he felt sorry for them because they were so stubborn. Then

2:23 went along: *It was the custom to let hungry travellers pick grains of wheat.*
3:2 Pharisees: *The Greek text has 'they', but see verse 6.*

he told the man, 'Stretch out your hand.' He did, and his bad
hand was healed.
6The Pharisees left. And straight away they started making
plans with Herod's followers to kill Jesus.

large crowds come to Jesus

7Jesus led his disciples down to the shore of the lake. Large
crowds followed him from Galilee, Judea, 8and Jerusalem.
People came from Idumea, as well as other places east of the
River Jordan. They also came from the region around the
cities of Tyre and Sidon. All these crowds came because they
had heard what Jesus was doing. 9He even had to tell his disciples to get a boat ready to keep him from being crushed by
the crowds.
10After Jesus had healed many people, the other sick
people begged him to let them touch him. 11And whenever
any evil spirits saw Jesus, they would fall to the ground and
shout, 'You are the Son of God!' 12But Jesus warned the spirits not to tell who he was.

Jesus chooses his twelve apostles

13Jesus decided to ask some of his disciples to go up on a
mountain with him, and they went. 14Then he chose twelve of
them to be his apostles, so that they could be with him. He
also wanted to send them out to preach 15and to force out
demons. 16Simon was one of the twelve, and Jesus named
him Peter. 17There were also James and John, the two sons
of Zebedee. Jesus called them Boanerges, which means
'Thunderbolts'. 18Andrew, Philip, Bartholomew, Matthew,
Thomas, James son of Alphaeus, and Thaddaeus were also

3:6 Herod's followers: *People who were political followers of the family of Herod the Great and his son Herod Antipas.*

apostles. The others were Simon, known as the Eager One,
[19]and Judas Iscariot, who later betrayed Jesus.

Jesus and the ruler of demons

[20]Jesus went back home, and once again such a large crowd
gathered that there was no chance even to eat. [21]When
Jesus' family heard what he was doing, they thought he was
mad and went to get him under control.

[22]Some teachers of the Law of Moses came from
Jerusalem and said, 'This man is under the power of Beelzebul, the ruler of demons! He is even forcing out demons with the help of Beelzebul.'

[23]Jesus told the people to gather around him. Then he spoke to them in riddles and said:

> How can Satan force himself out? [24]A nation whose
> people fight each other won't last very long. [25]And a fam-
> ily that fights won't last long either. [26]So if Satan fights
> against himself, that will be the end of him.
>
> [27]How can anyone break into the house of a strong man and steal his things, unless he first ties up the strong man? Then he can take everything.
>
> [28]I promise you that any of the sinful things you say or do can be forgiven, no matter how terrible those things
> are. [29]But if you speak against the Holy Spirit, you can
> never be forgiven. That sin will be held against you for ever.

[30]Jesus said this because the people were saying that he had an evil spirit in him.

3:18 known as the Eager One: *The Greek text has 'Cananaean', which probably comes from a Hebrew word meaning 'zealous' (see Luke 6.15). 'Zealot' was the name later given to the members of a Jewish group which resisted and fought against the Romans.*
3:19 Iscariot: *This may mean 'a man from Kerioth' (a place in Judea). But more probably it means 'a man who was a liar' or 'a man who was a betrayer'.*

Jesus' mother and brothers

31 Jesus' mother and brothers came and stood outside. Then
they sent someone with a message for him to come out to
them. 32 The crowd that was sitting around Jesus told him,
'Your mother and your brothers and sisters are outside and
want to see you.'
33 Jesus asked, 'Who is my mother and who are my brothers?' 34 Then he looked at the people sitting around him and
said, 'Here are my mother and my brothers. 35 Anyone who
obeys God is my brother or sister or mother.'

a story about a farmer

4 The next time Jesus taught beside Lake Galilee, a big
crowd gathered. It was so large that he had to sit in a
boat out on the lake, while the people stood on the
shore. 2 He used stories to teach them many things, and this
is part of what he taught:

> 3 Now listen! A farmer went out to scatter seed in a field.
> 4 While the farmer was scattering the seed, some of it fell
> along the road and was eaten by birds. 5 Other seeds fell
> on thin, rocky ground and quickly started growing because
> the soil wasn't very deep. 6 But when the sun came up, the
> plants were scorched and dried up, because they did not
> have enough roots. 7 Some other seeds fell where thorn
> bushes grew up and choked out the plants. So they did not
> produce any grain. 8 But a few seeds did fall on good
> ground where the plants grew and produced thirty or sixty
> or even a hundred times as much as was scattered.

9 Then Jesus said, 'If you have ears, pay attention.'

why Jesus used stories

10When Jesus was alone with the twelve apostles and some others, they asked him about these stories. 11He answered:

I have explained the secret about God's kingdom to you,
but for others I can use only stories. 12The reason is,

'These people will look and look, but never see.
They will listen and listen, but never understand.
If they did, they would turn to God,
and he would forgive them.'

Jesus explains the story about the farmer

13Jesus told them:

If you don't understand this story, you won't understand
any others. 14What the farmer is spreading is really the
message about the kingdom. 15The seeds that fell along
the road are the people who hear the message. But Satan
soon comes and snatches it away from them. 16The seeds
that fell on rocky ground are the people who gladly hear the
message and accept it straight away. 17But they don't have
any roots, and they don't last very long. As soon as life
gets hard or the message gets them in trouble, they give
up.

18The seeds that fell among the thorn bushes are also
people who hear the message. 19But they start worrying
about the needs of this life. They are fooled by the desire
to get rich and to have all kinds of other things. So the
message gets choked out, and they never produce anything. 20The seeds that fell on good ground are the people
who hear and welcome the message. They produce thirty
or sixty or even a hundred times as much as was planted.

light

21 Jesus also said:

You don't light a lamp and put it under a clay pot or
under a bed. Don't you put a lamp on a lampstand?
22 There is nothing hidden that will not be made public.
There is no secret that will not be well known. 23 If you have
ears, pay attention!

24 Listen carefully to what you hear! The way you treat
others will be the way you will be treated – and even worse.
25 Everyone who has something will be given more. But
people who don't have anything will lose what little they
have.

another story about seeds

26 Again Jesus said:

God's kingdom is like what happens when a farmer scat-
ters seed in a field. 27 The farmer sleeps at night and is up
and around during the day. Yet the seeds keep sprouting
and growing, and he doesn't understand how. 28 It is the
ground that makes the seeds sprout and grow into plants
that produce grain. 29 Then when harvest season comes
and the grain is ripe, the farmer cuts it with a sickle.

a mustard seed

30 Finally, Jesus said:

What is God's kingdom like? What story can I use to
explain it? 31 It is like what happens when a mustard seed
is planted in the ground. It is the smallest seed in all the
world. 32 But once it is planted, it grows larger than any

4:29 sickle: *A knife with a long curved blade, used to cut grain and other crops.*

garden plant. It even puts out branches that are big enough for birds to nest in its shade.

the reason for teaching with stories

[33]Jesus used many other stories when he spoke to the
people, and he taught them as much as they could understand. [34]He did not tell them anything without using stories.
But when he was alone with his disciples, he explained everything to them.

a storm

[35]That evening, Jesus said to his disciples, 'Let's cross to the
east side.' [36]So they left the crowd, and his disciples started
across the lake with him in the boat. Some other boats followed along. [37]Suddenly a storm struck the lake. Waves
started splashing into the boat, and it was about to sink.
[38]Jesus was in the back of the boat with his head on a pil-
low, and he was asleep. His disciples woke him and said,
'Teacher, don't you care that we're about to drown?'
[39]Jesus got up and ordered the wind and the waves to be
quiet. The wind stopped, and everything was calm.
[40]Jesus asked his disciples, 'Why were you afraid? Don't
you have any faith?'
[41]Now they were more afraid than ever and said to each
other, 'Who is this? Even the wind and the waves obey him!'

a man with evil spirits

5
Jesus and his disciples crossed Lake Galilee and
came to shore near the town of Gerasa. [2]When he was
getting out of the boat, a man with an evil spirit quickly
ran to him [3]from the graveyard where he had been living. No

5:3 graveyard: *It was thought that demons and evil spirits lived in graveyards.*

one was able to tie the man up any more, not even with a
chain. [4]He had often been put in chains and leg irons, but he
broke the chains and smashed the leg irons. No one could
control him. [5]Night and day he was in the graveyard or on the
hills, yelling and cutting himself with stones.

[6]When the man saw Jesus in the distance, he ran up to
him and knelt down. [7]He shouted, 'Jesus, Son of God in
heaven, what do you want with me? Promise me in God's
name that you won't torture me!' [8]The man said this because
Jesus had already told the evil spirit to come out of him.

[9]Jesus asked, 'What is your name?'

The man answered, 'My name is Lots, because I have
"lots" of evil spirits.' [10]He then begged Jesus not to send
them away.

[11]Over on the hillside a large herd of pigs was feeding.
[12]So the evil spirits begged Jesus, 'Send us into those pigs!
Let us go into them.' [13]Jesus let them go, and they went out
of the man and into the pigs. The whole herd of about two
thousand pigs rushed down the steep bank into the lake and
drowned.

[14]The men taking care of the pigs ran to the town and the
farms to spread the news. Then the people came out to see
what had happened. [15]When they came to Jesus, they saw the
man who had once been full of demons. He was sitting there
with his clothes on and in his right mind, and they were terrified.

[16]Everyone who had seen what had happened told about
the man and the pigs. [17]Then the people started begging
Jesus to leave their part of the country.

[18]When Jesus was getting into the boat, the man begged
to go with him. [19]But Jesus would not let him. Instead, he
said, 'Go home to your family and tell them how much the
Lord has done for you and how good he has been to you.'

[20]The man went away into the region near the ten cities

5:20 the ten cities known as Decapolis: *A group of ten cities east of Samaria and Galilee, where the people followed the Greek way of life.*

known as Decapolis and began telling everyone how much Jesus had done for him. Everyone who heard what had happened was amazed.

a dying girl and a sick woman

21Once again Jesus got into the boat and crossed Lake
Galilee. Then as he stood on the shore, a large crowd gathered around him. 22The person in charge of the Jewish meeting place was also there. His name was Jairus, and when he
saw Jesus, he went over to him. He knelt at Jesus' feet 23and
started begging him for help. He said, 'My daughter is about
to die! Please come and touch her, so she will get well and
live.' 24Jesus went with Jairus. Many people followed along
and kept crowding around.

25In the crowd was a woman who had been bleeding for
twelve years. 26She had gone to many doctors, and they had
not done anything except cause her a lot of pain. She had
paid them all the money she had. But instead of getting better, she only got worse.

27The woman had heard about Jesus, so she came up
behind him in the crowd and barely touched his clothes.
28She had said to herself, 'If I can just touch his clothes, I will
get well.' 29As soon as she touched them, her bleeding
stopped, and she knew she was well.

30At that moment Jesus felt power go out from him. He
turned to the crowd and asked, 'Who touched my clothes?'

31His disciples said to him, 'Look at all these people
crowding around you! How can you ask who touched you?'
32But Jesus turned to see who had touched him.

33The woman knew what had happened to her. She came
shaking with fear and knelt down in front of Jesus. Then she
told him the whole story.

34Jesus said to the woman, 'You are now well because of

5:21 crossed Lake Galilee: *To the west side.*

your faith. May God give you peace! You are healed, and you will no longer be in pain.'

35While Jesus was still speaking, some men came from Jairus' home and said, 'Your daughter has died! Why bother the teacher any more?'

36Jesus heard what they said, and he said to Jairus, 'Don't worry. Just have faith!'

37Jesus did not let anyone go with him except Peter and the two brothers, James and John. 38They went home with Jairus and saw the people crying and making a lot of noise. 39Then Jesus went inside and said to them, 'Why are you crying and carrying on like this? The child isn't dead. She is just asleep.' 40But the people laughed at him.

After Jesus had sent them all out of the house, he took the girl's father and mother and his three disciples and went to where she was. 41–42He took the twelve-year-old girl by the hand and said, 'Talitha, koum!' which means, 'Little girl, get up!' The girl got straight up and started walking around.

Everyone was greatly surprised. 43But Jesus ordered them not to tell anyone what had happened. Then he said, 'Give her something to eat.'

the people of Nazareth turn against Jesus

6 Jesus left and returned to his home town with his disciples. 2The next Sabbath he taught in the Jewish meeting place. Many of the people who heard him were amazed and asked, 'How can he do all this? Where did he get such wisdom and the power to perform these miracles? 3Isn't he the carpenter, the son of Mary? Aren't

5:38 crying and making a lot of noise: *The Jewish people often hired mourners for funerals.*

5:41–42 Talitha, koum: *These words are in Aramaic, a language spoken in Palestine during the time of Jesus.*

6:1 home town: *Nazareth.*

James, Joseph, Judas, and Simon his brothers? Don't his sisters still live here in our town?' The people were very unhappy because of what he was doing.

4But Jesus said, 'Prophets are honoured by everyone, except the people of their home town and their relatives and their own family.' 5Jesus could not perform any miracles there, except to heal a few sick people by placing his hands on them. 6He was surprised that the people did not have any faith.

instructions for the twelve apostles

Jesus taught in all the neighbouring villages. 7Then he called together his twelve apostles and sent them out two by two with power over evil spirits. 8He told them, 'You may take along a walking stick. But don't carry food or a travelling bag or any money. 9It's all right to wear sandals, but don't take along a change of clothes. 10When you are welcomed into a home, stay there until you leave that town. 11If any place won't welcome you or listen to your message, leave and shake the dust from your feet as a warning to them.'

12The apostles left and started telling everyone to turn to God. 13They forced out many demons and healed a lot of sick people by putting olive oil on them.

the death of John the Baptist

14Jesus became so well-known that Herod the ruler heard about him. Some people thought he was John the Baptist, who had come back to life with the power to perform mir-

6:11 shake the dust from your feet: *This was a way of showing rejection.*
6:13 olive oil: *The Jewish people used olive oil as a way of healing people. Sometimes olive oil is a symbol for healing by means of a miracle (see James 5:14).*
6:14 Herod the ruler: *Herod Antipas, the son of Herod the Great.*

acles. 15Others thought he was Elijah or some other prophet
who had lived long ago. 16But when Herod heard about Jesus,
he said, 'This must be John! I had his head cut off, and now
he has come back to life.'

17–18Herod had earlier married Herodias, the wife of his
brother Philip. But John had told him, 'It isn't right for you to
take your brother's wife!' So, in order to please Herodias,
Herod arrested John and put him in prison.

19Herodias had a grudge against John and wanted to kill
him. But she could not do it 20because Herod was afraid of
John and protected him. He knew that John was a good and
holy man. Even though Herod was confused by what John
said, he was glad to listen to him. And he often did.

21Finally, Herodias got her chance when Herod gave a
great birthday celebration for himself and invited his officials,
his army officers, and the leaders of Galilee. 22The daughter
of Herodias came in and danced for Herod and his guests.
She pleased them so much that Herod said, 'Ask for anything, and it's yours! 23I swear that I will give you as much as
half of my kingdom, if you want it.'

24The girl left and asked her mother, 'What do you think I
should ask for?'

Her mother answered, 'The head of John the Baptist!'

25The girl hurried back and told Herod, 'Straight away on a
dish I want the head of John the Baptist!'

26The king was very sorry for what he had said. But he did
not want to break the promise he had made in front of his
guests. 27At once he ordered a guard to cut off John's head
there in prison. 28The guard put the head on a dish and took
it to the girl. Then she gave it to her mother.

29When John's followers learnt that he had been killed,
they took his body and put it in a tomb.

6:15 Elijah: *Many of the Jewish people expected the prophet Elijah to come and prepare the way for the Messiah.*

Jesus feeds five thousand

[30]After the apostles returned to Jesus, they told him everything they had done and taught. [31]But so many people were
coming and going that Jesus and the apostles did not even
have a chance to eat. Then Jesus said, 'Let's go to a place
where we can be alone and get some rest.' [32]They left in a
boat for a place where they could be alone. [33]But many
people saw them leave and worked out where they were going.
So people from every town ran on ahead and got there first.

[34]When Jesus got out of the boat, he saw the large crowd
that was like sheep without a shepherd. He felt sorry for the
people and started teaching them many things.

[35]That evening the disciples came to Jesus and said, 'This
place is like a desert, and it is already late. [36]Let the crowds
leave, so they can go to the farms and villages near here and
buy something to eat.'

[37]Jesus replied, 'You give them something to eat.'

But they asked him, 'Don't you know that it would take almost a year's wages to buy all these people something to eat?'

[38]Then Jesus said, 'How much bread do you have? Go and see!'

They found out and answered, 'We have five small loaves
of bread and two fish.' [39]Jesus told his disciples to make the
people sit down on the green grass. [40]They sat down in
groups of a hundred and groups of fifty.

[41]Jesus took the five loaves and the two fish. He looked up towards heaven and blessed the food. Then he broke the bread and handed it to his disciples to give to the people. He

6:30 the apostles returned to Jesus: *From the mission on which he had sent them (see 6:7, 12, 13).*

6:31 a place: *This was probably north-east of Lake Galilee (see verse 45).*

6:37 almost a year's wages: *The Greek text has 'two hundred silver coins'. Each coin was the average day's wage for a worker.*

6:38 small loaves of bread: *These would have been flat and round or in the shape of a bun.*

also divided the two fish, so that everyone could have some.
42After everyone had eaten all they wanted, 43Jesus' disciples picked up twelve large baskets of leftover bread and
fish.
44There were five thousand men who ate the food.

Jesus walks on the water

45Straight away, Jesus made his disciples get into the boat
and start back across to Bethsaida. But he stayed until he
had sent the crowds away. 46Then he said goodbye to them
and went up on the side of a mountain to pray.
47Later that evening he was still there by himself, and the
boat was somewhere in the middle of the lake. 48He could
see that the disciples were struggling hard, because they
were rowing against the wind. Not long before morning, Jesus
came towards them. He was walking on the water and was
about to pass the boat.
49When the disciples saw Jesus walking on the water, they
thought he was a ghost, and they started screaming. 50All of
them saw him and were terrified. But at that same time he
said, 'Don't worry! I am Jesus. Don't be afraid.' 51He then got
into the boat with them, and the wind died down. The disciples were completely confused. 52Their minds were closed,
and they could not understand the true meaning of the loaves
of bread.

Jesus heals sick people in Gennesaret

53Jesus and his disciples crossed the lake and brought the
boat to shore near the town of Gennesaret. 54As soon as they
got out of the boat, the people recognized Jesus. 55So they
ran all over that part of the country to bring their sick people
to him on mats. They brought them each time they heard
where he was. 56In every village or farm or market place
where Jesus went, the people brought their sick to him. They

begged him to let them just touch his clothes, and everyone
who did was healed.

the teaching of the ancestors

7 Some Pharisees and several teachers of the Law of
Moses from Jerusalem came and gathered around
Jesus. [2]They noticed that some of his disciples ate
without first washing their hands.
[3]The Pharisees and many other Jewish people obey the
teachings of their ancestors. They always wash their hands in
the proper way before eating. [4]None of them will eat anything
they buy in the market until it is washed. They also follow a
lot of other teachings, such as washing cups, jugs, and
bowls.
[5]The Pharisees and teachers asked Jesus, 'Why don't your
disciples obey what our ancestors taught us to do? Why do
they eat without washing their hands?'
[6]Jesus replied:

You are nothing but show-offs! The prophet Isaiah was
right when he wrote that God had said,

'All of you praise me with your words,
but you never really think about me.
[7]It is useless for you to worship me,
when you teach rules made up by humans.'

[8]You disobey God's commands in order to obey what
humans have taught. [9]You are good at rejecting God's
commands so that you can follow your own teachings!
[10]Didn't Moses command you to respect your father and
mother? Didn't he tell you to put to death all who curse

***7:2 without first washing their hands:** The Jewish people had strict laws about washing their hands before eating, especially if they had been out in public.*

their parents? [11]But you let people get by without helping
their parents when they should. You let them say that what
they own has been offered to God. [12]You won't let those
people help their parents. [13]And you ignore God's commands in order to follow your own teaching. You do a lot of
other things that are just as bad.

what really makes people unclean

[14]Jesus called the crowd together again and said, 'Pay attention and try to understand what I mean. [15–16]The food that
you put into your mouth doesn't make you unclean and unfit
to worship God. The bad words that come out of your mouth
are what make you unclean.'

[17]After Jesus and his disciples had left the crowd and had
gone into the house, they asked him what these sayings
meant. [18]He answered, 'Don't you know what I am talking
about by now? Surely you know that the food you put into your
mouth cannot make you unclean. [19]It doesn't go into your
heart, but into your stomach, and then out of your body.' By
saying this, Jesus meant that all foods were fit to eat.

[20]Then Jesus said:

> What comes from your heart is what makes you
> unclean. [21]Out of your heart come evil thoughts, vulgar
> deeds, stealing, murder, [22]unfaithfulness in marriage,
> greed, meanness, deceit, indecency, envy, insults, pride,
> and foolishness. [23]All these come from your heart, and
> they are what make you unfit to worship God.

a woman's faith

[24]Jesus left and went to the region near the city of Tyre,

7:11 has been offered to God: *According to Jewish custom, when anything was offered to God, it could not be used for anyone else, not even for a person's parents.*

where he stayed in someone's home. He did not want people
to know he was there, but they found out anyway. 25A woman
whose daughter had an evil spirit in her heard where Jesus
was. And straight away she came and knelt down at his feet.
26The woman was Greek and had been born in the part of
Syria known as Phoenicia. She begged Jesus to force the
demon out of her daughter. 27But Jesus said, 'The children
must first be fed! It isn't right to take away their food and feed
it to dogs.'

28The woman replied, 'Lord, even dogs eat the crumbs that
children drop from the table.'

29Jesus answered, 'That's true! You may go now. The
demon has left your daughter.' 30When the woman got back
home, she found her child lying on the bed. The demon had
gone.

Jesus heals a man who was deaf and could hardly talk

31Jesus left the region around Tyre and went by way of Sidon
towards Lake Galilee. He went through the land near the ten
cities known as Decapolis. 32Some people brought to him a
man who was deaf and could hardly talk. They begged Jesus
just to touch him.

33After Jesus had taken him aside from the crowd, he
stuck his fingers in the man's ears. Then he spat and put the
spit on the man's tongue. 34Jesus looked up towards heaven,
and with a groan he said, 'Effatha!' which means 'Open up!'
35At once the man could hear, and he had no more trouble
talking clearly.

36Jesus told the people not to say anything about what he

7:27 feed it to dogs: *The Jewish people often referred to Gentiles as dogs.*
7:31 the ten cities known as Decapolis: *See the note at 5:20.*
7:34 Effatha: *This word is in Aramaic, a language spoken in Palestine during the time of Jesus.*

had done. But the more he told them, the more they talked about it. [37]They were completely amazed and said, 'Everything he does is good! He even heals people who cannot hear or talk.'

Jesus feeds four thousand

8 One day another large crowd gathered around Jesus. They had not brought along anything to eat. So Jesus called his disciples together and said, [2]'I feel sorry for these people. They have been with me for three days, and they don't have anything to eat. [3]Some of them live a long way from here. If I send them away hungry, they might faint on their way home.'

[4]The disciples said, 'This place is like a desert. Where can we find enough food to feed such a crowd?'

[5]Jesus asked them how much food they had. They replied, 'Seven small loaves of bread.'

[6]After Jesus told the crowd to sit down, he took the seven loaves and blessed them. He then broke the loaves and handed them to his disciples, who passed them out to the crowd. [7]They also had a few little fish, and after Jesus had blessed these, he told the disciples to pass them around.

[8–9]The crowd of about four thousand people ate all they wanted, and the leftovers filled seven large baskets.

As soon as Jesus had sent the people away, [10]he got into the boat with the disciples and crossed to the territory near Dalmanutha.

a sign from heaven

[11]The Pharisees came out and started an argument with Jesus. They wanted to test him by asking for a sign from

8:5 small loaves of bread: *See the note at 6:38.*
8:10 Dalmanutha: *The place is unknown.*

heaven. 12Jesus groaned and said, 'Why are you always looking for a sign? I can promise you that you will not be given one!' 13Then he left them. He again got into a boat and crossed over to the other side of the lake.

the yeast of the Pharisees and of Herod

14The disciples had forgotten to bring any bread, and they had only one loaf with them in the boat. 15Jesus warned them, 'Watch out! Guard against the yeast of the Pharisees and of Herod.'

16The disciples talked this over and said to each other, 'He must be saying this because we don't have any bread.'

17Jesus knew what they were thinking and asked, 'Why are you talking about not having any bread? Don't you understand? Are your minds still closed? 18Are your eyes blind and your ears deaf? Don't you remember 19how many baskets of leftovers you picked up when I fed those five thousand people with only five small loaves of bread?'

'Yes,' the disciples answered. 'There were twelve baskets.'

20Jesus then asked, 'And how many baskets of leftovers did you pick up when I broke seven small loaves of bread for those four thousand people?'

'Seven,' they answered.

21'Don't you know what I am talking about by now?' Jesus asked.

Jesus heals a blind man at Bethsaida

22As Jesus and his disciples were going into Bethsaida, some people brought a blind man to him and begged him to touch the man. 23Jesus took him by the hand and led him out of the

8:15 Herod: *Herod Antipas, the son of Herod the Great.*

village, where he spat into the man's eyes. He placed his hands on the blind man and asked him if he could see anything. 24The man looked up and said, 'I see people, but they look like trees walking around.'

25Once again Jesus placed his hands on the man's eyes, and this time the man stared. His eyes were healed, and he saw everything clearly. 26Jesus said to him, 'You may return home now, but don't go into the village.'

who is Jesus?

27Jesus and his disciples went to the villages near the town of Caesarea Philippi. As they were walking along, he asked them, 'What do people say about me?'

28The disciples answered, 'Some say you are John the Baptist or perhaps Elijah. Others say you are one of the prophets.'

29Then Jesus asked them, 'But who do you say I am?'

'You are the Messiah!' Peter replied.

30Jesus warned the disciples not to tell anyone about him.

Jesus speaks about his suffering and death

31Jesus began telling his disciples what would happen to him. He said, 'The nation's leaders, the chief priests, and the teachers of the Law of Moses will make the Son of Man suffer terribly. He will be rejected and killed, but three days later he will rise to life.' 32Then Jesus explained clearly what he meant.

Peter took Jesus aside and told him to stop talking like that. 33But when Jesus turned and saw the disciples, he corrected Peter. He said to him, 'Satan, get away from me! You are thinking like everyone else and not like God.'

8:28 Elijah: *See the note at 6:15.*

34 Jesus then told the crowd and the disciples to come
closer, and he said:

If any of you want to be my followers, you must forget
about yourself. You must take up your cross and follow me.
35 If you want to save your life, you will destroy it. But if you
give up your life for me and for the good news, you will save
it. 36 What will you gain, if you own the whole world but
destroy yourself? 37 What could you give to get back your
soul?

38 Don't be ashamed of me and my message among
these unfaithful and sinful people! If you are, the Son of
Man will be ashamed of you when he comes in the glory of
his Father with the holy angels.

I can assure you that some of the people standing
here will not die before they see God's kingdom 9
come with power.

the true glory of Jesus

2 Six days later Jesus took Peter, James, and John with him.
They went up on a high mountain, where they could be alone.
There in front of the disciples, Jesus was completely
changed. 3 And his clothes became much whiter than any
bleach on earth could make them. 4 Then Moses and Elijah
were there talking with Jesus.

5 Peter said to Jesus, 'Teacher, it is good for us to be here!
Let us make three shelters, one for you, one for Moses,
and one for Elijah.' 6 But Peter and the others were terribly
frightened, and he did not know what he was talking
about.

7 The shadow of a cloud passed over and covered them.
From the cloud a voice said, 'This is my Son, and I love him.
Listen to what he says!' 8 At once the disciples looked around,
but they saw only Jesus.

9 As Jesus and his disciples were coming down the moun-

tain, he told them not to say a word about what they had
seen, until the Son of Man had been raised from death. 10So
they kept it to themselves. But they wondered what he meant
by the words 'raised from death'.
11The disciples asked Jesus, 'Don't the teachers of the
Law of Moses say that Elijah must come before the Messiah
does?'
12Jesus answered:

> Elijah certainly will come to get everything ready. But
> don't the Scriptures also say that the Son of Man must suf-
> fer terribly and be rejected? 13I can assure you that Elijah
> has already come. And people treated him just as they
> wanted to, as the Scriptures say they would.

Jesus heals a boy

14When Jesus and his three disciples came back down, they
saw a large crowd around the other disciples. The teachers of
the Law of Moses were arguing with them.
15The crowd was really surprised to see Jesus, and everyone hurried over to greet him.
16Jesus asked, 'What are you arguing about?'
17Someone from the crowd answered, 'Teacher, I brought
my son to you. A demon keeps him from talking. 18Whenever
the demon attacks my son, it throws him to the ground and
makes him foam at the mouth and grit his teeth in pain. Then
he becomes stiff. I asked your disciples to force out the
demon, but they couldn't do it.'
19Jesus said, 'You people don't have any faith! How much
longer must I be with you? Why do I have to put up with you?
Bring the boy to me.'
20They brought the boy, and as soon as the demon saw
Jesus, it made the boy shake all over. He fell down and began

9:12 Elijah certainly will come: *See the note at 6:15.*

rolling on the ground and foaming at the mouth.

21 Jesus asked the boy's father, 'How long has he been like this?'

The man answered, 'Ever since he was a child.
22 The demon has often tried to kill him by throwing him into a fire or into water. Please have pity and help us if you can!'

23 Jesus replied, 'Why do you say "if you can"? Anything is possible for someone who has faith!'

24 Straight away the boy's father shouted, 'I do have faith! Please help me to have even more.'

25 When Jesus saw that a crowd was gathering fast, he spoke sternly to the evil spirit that had kept the boy from speaking or hearing. He said, 'I order you to come out of the boy! Don't ever bother him again.'

26 The spirit screamed and made the boy shake all over. Then it went out of him. The boy looked dead, and almost everyone said he was.
27 But Jesus took hold of his hand and helped him stand up.

28 After Jesus and the disciples had gone back home and were alone, they asked him, 'Why couldn't we force out that demon?'

29 Jesus answered, 'Only prayer can force out that kind of demon.'

Jesus again speaks about his death

30 Jesus left with his disciples and started through Galilee. He did not want anyone to know about it,
31 because he was teaching the disciples that the Son of Man would be handed over to people who would kill him. But three days later he would rise to life.
32 The disciples did not understand what Jesus meant, and they were afraid to ask.

who is the greatest?

33 Jesus and his disciples went to his home in Capernaum.

After they were inside the house, Jesus asked them, 'What were you arguing about along the way?' [34]They had been arguing about which one of them was the greatest, and so they did not answer.

[35]After Jesus sat down and told the twelve disciples to gather around him, he said, 'If you want the place of honour, you must become a slave and serve others!'

[36]Then Jesus made a child stand near him. He put his arm around the child and said, [37] 'When you welcome even a child because of me, you welcome me. And when you welcome me, you welcome the one who sent me.'

for or against Jesus

[38]John said, 'Teacher, we saw a man using your name to force demons out of people. But he wasn't one of us, and we told him to stop.'

[39]Jesus said to his disciples:

> Don't stop him! No one who performs miracles in my name is going to say something bad about me the next minute. [40]Anyone who isn't against us is for us. [41]And anyone who gives you a cup of water in my name, just because you belong to me, will surely be rewarded.

temptations to sin

Jesus continued:

> [42]It will be terrible for people who cause even one of my little followers to sin. Those people would be better off thrown into the sea with a heavy stone tied around their necks. [43–44]So if your hand causes you to sin, cut it off! You would be better off to go into life crippled than to have two hands and be thrown into the fires of hell that never go out. [45–46]If your foot causes you to sin, chop it off. You

would be better off to go into life lame than to have two
feet and be thrown into hell. [47]If your eye causes you to
sin, get rid of it. You would be better off to go into God's
kingdom with only one eye than to have two eyes and be
thrown into hell. [48]The worms there never die, and the fire
never stops burning.
[49]Everyone must be salted with fire.
[50]Salt is good. But if it no longer tastes like salt, how
can it be made salty again? Have salt among you and live
at peace with each other.

Jesus goes from Galilee to Jerusalem

teaching about divorce

10

After Jesus left, he went to Judea and then on
to the other side of the River Jordan. Once
again large crowds came to him, and as usual, he
taught them.
[2]Some Pharisees wanted to test Jesus. So they came up
to him and asked if it was right for a man to divorce his wife.
[3]Jesus asked them, 'What does the Law of Moses say about
that?'
[4]They answered, 'Moses allows a man to write out divorce
papers and send his wife away.'
[5]Jesus replied, 'Moses gave you this law because you are
so heartless. [6]But in the beginning God made a man and a
woman. [7]That's why a man leaves his father and mother and
gets married. [8]He becomes like one person with his wife.
Then they are no longer two people, but one. [9]And no one

9:49 salted with fire: *Some manuscripts add 'and every sacrifice will be seasoned with salt'. The verse may mean that Christ's followers must suffer because of their faith.*
9:50 Have salt among you and live at peace with each other: *This may mean that when Christ's followers have to suffer because of their faith, they must still try to live at peace with each other.*

should separate a couple that God has joined together.'
10 When Jesus and his disciples were back in the house,
they asked him about what he had said. 11He told them, 'A
man who divorces his wife and marries someone else is
unfaithful to his wife. 12A woman who divorces her husband
and marries again is also unfaithful.'

Jesus blesses little children

13Some people brought their children to Jesus so that he
could bless them by placing his hands on them. But his disciples told the people to stop bothering him.
14When Jesus saw this, he became angry and said, 'Let
the children come to me! Don't try to stop them. People who
are like these little children belong to the kingdom of God.
15I promise you that you cannot get into God's kingdom,
unless you accept it the way a child does.' 16Then Jesus took
the children in his arms and blessed them by placing his
hands on them.

a rich man

17As Jesus was walking down a road, a man ran up to him.
He knelt down, and asked, 'Good teacher, what can I do to
have eternal life?'
18Jesus replied, 'Why do you call me good? Only God is
good. 19You know the commandments. "Do not murder. Be
faithful in marriage. Do not steal. Do not tell lies about
others. Do not cheat. Respect your father and mother." '
20The man answered, 'Teacher, I have obeyed all these
commandments since I was a young man.'
21Jesus looked closely at the man. He liked him and said,
'There's one thing you still need to do. Go and sell everything

10:12 A woman who divorces her husband: *Roman law let a woman divorce her husband, but Jewish law did not let a woman do this.*

you own. Give the money to the poor, and you will have riches in heaven. Then come with me.'

22When the man heard Jesus say this, he went away gloomy and sad because he was very rich.

23Jesus looked around and said to his disciples, 'It's hard
for rich people to get into God's kingdom!' 24The disciples
were shocked to hear this. So Jesus told them again, 'It's terribly hard to get into God's kingdom! 25In fact, it's easier for
a camel to go through the eye of a needle than for a rich person to get into God's kingdom.'

26Jesus' disciples were even more amazed. They asked each other, 'How can anyone ever be saved?'

27Jesus looked at them and said, 'There are some things that people cannot do, but God can do anything.'

28Peter replied, 'Remember, we left everything to be your followers!'

29Jesus told him:

> You can be sure that anyone who gives up home or brothers or sisters or mother or father or children or land for me
> and for the good news 30will be rewarded. In this world they
> will be given a hundred times as many houses and brothers and sisters and mothers and children and pieces of land, though they will also be ill-treated. And in the world to come,
> they will have eternal life. 31But many who are now first will
> be last, and many who are now last will be first.

Jesus again tells about his death

32The disciples were confused as Jesus led them towards Jerusalem, and his other followers were afraid. Once again, Jesus took the twelve disciples aside and told them what was going to happen to him. He said:

> 33We are now on our way to Jerusalem where the Son of

Man will be handed over to the chief priests and the teachers of the Law of Moses. They will sentence him to death and hand him over to foreigners, [34]who will make fun of him and spit on him. They will beat him and kill him. But three days later he will rise to life.

the request of James and John

[35]James and John, the sons of Zebedee, came up to Jesus and asked, 'Teacher, will you do us a favour?'

[36]Jesus asked them what they wanted, [37]and they answered, 'When you come into your glory, please let one of us sit at your right side and the other at your left.'

[38]Jesus told them, 'You don't really know what you're asking! Are you able to drink from the cup that I must soon drink from or be baptized as I must be baptized?'

[39]'Yes, we are!' James and John answered.

Then Jesus replied, 'You certainly will drink from the cup from which I must drink. And you will be baptized just as I must! [40]But it isn't for me to say who will sit at my right side and at my left. That is for God to decide.'

[41]When the ten other disciples heard this, they were angry with James and John. [42]But Jesus called the disciples together and said:

> You know that those foreigners who call themselves kings like to order their people around. And their great leaders have full power over the people they rule. [43]But don't act like them. If you want to be great, you must be the servant of all the others. [44]And if you want to be first, you must be everyone's slave. [45]The Son of Man did not

10:33 foreigners: *The Romans who ruled Judea at this time.*

10:37 right side ... left: *The most powerful people in a kingdom sat at the right and left side of the king.*

10:38 drink from the cup: *In the Scriptures a 'cup' is sometimes used as a symbol of suffering. To 'drink from the cup' would be to suffer.*

come to be a slave master, but a slave who will give his life
to rescue many people.

Jesus heals blind Bartimaeus

[46]Jesus and his disciples went to Jericho. And as they were
leaving, they were followed by a large crowd. A blind beggar
called Bartimaeus son of Timaeus was sitting beside the
road. [47]When he heard that it was Jesus from Nazareth, he
shouted, 'Jesus, Son of David, have pity on me!' [48]Many
people told the man to stop, but he shouted even louder,
'Son of David, have pity on me!'

[49]Jesus stopped and said, 'Call him over!'

They called out to the blind man and said, 'Don't be afraid!
Come on! He is calling for you.' [50]The man threw off his coat
as he jumped up and ran to Jesus.

[51]Jesus asked, 'What do you want me to do for you?' The
blind man answered, 'Master, I want to see!'

[52]Jesus told him, 'You may go. Your eyes are healed
because of your faith.'

Straight away the man could see, and he went down the
road with Jesus.

Jesus' last week: his trial and death

Jesus enters Jerusalem

11

Jesus and his disciples reached Bethphage and
Bethany near the Mount of Olives. When they were getting close to Jerusalem, Jesus sent two of them on
ahead. [2]He told them, 'Go into the next village. As soon as
you enter it, you will find a young donkey that has never been

10:45 rescue: *The Greek word often, though not always, means the payment of a price to free a slave or a prisoner.*

10:47 Son of David: *The Jewish people expected the Messiah to be from the family of King David, and for this reason the Messiah was often called the 'Son of David'.*

ridden. Untie the donkey and bring it here. 3If anyone asks
why you are doing that, say, "The Lord needs it and will soon
bring it back." '

4The disciples left and found the donkey tied near a door
that faced the street. While they were untying it, 5some of the
people standing there asked, 'Why are you untying the donkey?' 6They told them what Jesus had said, and the people
let them take it. 7The disciples led the donkey to Jesus. They
put some of their clothes on its back, and Jesus got on.
8Many people spread clothes on the road, while others went
to cut branches from the fields.

9In front of Jesus and behind him, people went along
shouting,

'Hooray! God bless the one
who comes in the name of the Lord!
10God bless the coming kingdom of our ancestor David.
Hooray for God in heaven above!'

11After Jesus had gone to Jerusalem, he went into the temple and looked around at everything. But since it was already late in the day, he went back to Bethany with the twelve disciples.

Jesus puts a curse on a fig tree

12When Jesus and his disciples left Bethany the next morning, he was hungry. 13From a distance Jesus saw a fig tree
covered with leaves, and he went to see if there were any figs
on the tree. But there were not any, because it wasn't the
season for figs. 14So Jesus said to the tree, 'Never again will

11:8 spread ... branches from the fields: *This was one way that the Jewish people welcomed a famous person.*

11:9 Hooray: *This translates a word that can mean 'please save us'. But it is most often used as a shout of praise to God.*

anyone eat fruit from this tree!' The disciples heard him say
this.

Jesus in the temple

15After Jesus and his disciples reached Jerusalem, he went
into the temple and began chasing out everyone who was
selling and buying. He turned over the tables of the money-
changers and the benches of those who were selling doves.
16Jesus would not let anyone carry things through the temple.
17Then he taught the people and said, 'The Scriptures
say, "My house should be called a place of worship for
all nations." But you have made it a place where robbers
hide!'
18The chief priests and the teachers of the Law of Moses
heard what Jesus said, and they started looking for a way to
kill him. They were afraid of him, because the crowds were
completely amazed at his teaching.
19That evening, Jesus and the disciples went outside the
city.

a lesson from the fig tree

20As the disciples walked past the fig tree the next morning,
they noticed that it was completely dried up, roots and all.
21Peter remembered what Jesus had said to the tree. Then
Peter said, 'Teacher, look! The tree you put a curse on has
dried up.'

22Jesus told his disciples:

Have faith in God! 23If you have faith in God and don't
doubt, you can tell this mountain to get up and jump into
the sea, and it will. 24Everything you ask for in prayer will
be yours, if you only have faith.
25–26Whenever you stand up to pray, you must forgive

what others have done to you. Then your Father in heaven will forgive your sins.

a question about Jesus' authority

27 Jesus and his disciples returned to Jerusalem. And as he was walking through the temple, the chief priests, the nation's leaders, and the teachers of the Law of Moses came over to him. 28 They asked, 'What right do you have to do these things? Who gave you this authority?'

29 Jesus answered, 'I have just one question to ask you. If you answer it, I will tell you where I got the right to do these things. 30 Who gave John the right to baptize? Was it God in heaven or merely some human being?'

31 They thought it over and said to each other, 'We can't say that God gave John this right. Jesus will ask us why we didn't believe John. 32 On the other hand, these people think that John was a prophet. So we can't say that it was merely some human who gave John the right to baptize.'

They were afraid of the crowd 33 and told Jesus, 'We don't know.'

Jesus replied, 'Then I won't tell you who gave me the right to do what I do.'

tenants of a vineyard

12 Jesus then told them this story:

A farmer once planted a vineyard. He built a wall around it and dug a pit to crush the grapes in. He also built a look-out tower. Then he let his vineyard and left the country.

2 When it was harvest time, he sent a servant to get his share of the grapes. 3 The tenants grabbed the servant. They beat him up and sent him away without a thing.

4 The owner sent another servant, but the tenants beat

him on the head and insulted him terribly. 5Then the man
sent another servant, and they killed him. He kept sending
servant after servant. They beat some of them and killed
others.

6The owner had a son he loved very much. Finally, he
sent his son to the tenants because he thought they would
respect him. 7But they said to themselves, 'Some day he
will own this vineyard. Let's kill him! That way we can have
it all for ourselves.' 8So they grabbed the owner's son and
killed him. Then they threw his body out of the vineyard.

9Jesus asked, 'What do you think the owner of the vineyard
will do? He will come and kill those tenants and let someone
else have his vineyard. 10Surely you know that the Scriptures
say,

> "The stone that the builders tossed aside
> is now the most important stone of all.
> 11This is something the Lord has done,
> and it is amazing to us." '

12The leaders knew that Jesus was really talking about
them, and they wanted to arrest him. But because they were
afraid of the crowd, they let him alone and left.

paying taxes

13The Pharisees got together with Herod's followers. Then
they sent some men to trick Jesus into saying something
wrong. 14They went to him and said, 'Teacher, we know that
you are honest. You treat everyone with the same respect, no
matter who they are. And you teach the truth about what God

12:13 Herod's followers: *People who were political followers of the family of Herod the Great and his son Herod Antipas.*

wants people to do. Tell us, should we pay taxes to the Emperor or not?'

[15]Jesus knew what they were up to, and he said, 'Why are you trying to test me? Show me a coin!'

[16]They brought him a silver coin, and he asked, 'Whose picture and name are on it?'

'The Emperor's,' they answered.

[17]Then Jesus told them, 'Give the Emperor what belongs to him and give God what belongs to God.' The men were amazed at Jesus.

life in the future world

[18]The Sadducees did not believe that people would rise to life after death. So some of them came to Jesus and said:

> [19]Teacher, Moses wrote that if a married man dies and has no children, his brother should marry the widow. Their first son would then be thought of as the son of the dead brother. [20]There were once seven brothers. The first one married, but died without having any children. [21]The second brother married his brother's widow, and he also died without having children. The same thing happened to the third brother, [22]and finally to all seven brothers. At last the woman died. [23]When God raises people from death, whose wife will this woman be? After all, she had been married to all seven brothers.

[24]Jesus answered:

> You are completely wrong! You don't know what the Scriptures teach. And you don't know anything about the power of God. [25]When God raises people to life, they won't marry. They will be like the angels in heaven. [26]You know about people being raised to life. You know that in the

story about Moses and the burning bush, God said, 'I am the God worshipped by Abraham, Isaac, and Jacob.' 27He isn't the God of the dead, but of the living. You Sadducees are all wrong.

the most important commandment

28One of the teachers of the Law of Moses came up while Jesus and the Sadducees were arguing. When he heard Jesus give a good answer, he asked him, 'What is the most important commandment?'

29Jesus answered, 'The most important one says: "People of Israel, you have only one Lord and God. 30You must love him with all your heart, soul, mind, and strength." 31The second most important commandment says: "Love others as much as you love yourself." No other commandment is more important than these.'

32The man replied, 'Teacher, you are certainly right to say there is only one God. 33It is also true that we must love God with all our heart, mind, and strength, and that we must love others as much as we love ourselves. These commandments are more important than all the sacrifices and offerings that we could possibly make.'

34When Jesus saw that the man had given a sensible answer, he told him, 'You are not far from God's kingdom.' After this, no one dared ask Jesus any more questions.

about David's son

35As Jesus was teaching in the temple, he said, 'How can the teachers of the Law of Moses say that the Messiah will come from the family of King David? 36The Holy Spirit led David to say,

12:26 'I am the God worshipped by Abraham, Isaac, and Jacob': *Jesus argues that if God is worshipped by these three, they must still be alive, because he is the God of the living.*

'The Lord said to my Lord:
Sit at my right side
until I make your enemies into a footstool for you.'

37 If David called the Messiah his Lord, how can the Messiah be his son?'

The large crowd enjoyed listening to Jesus teach.

Jesus condemns the Pharisees and the teachers of the Law of Moses

38 As Jesus was teaching, he said:

Guard against the teachers of the Law of Moses! They love to walk around in long robes and be greeted in the market.
39 They like the front seats in the meeting places and the best seats at banquets.
40 But they cheat widows out of their homes and pray long prayers just to show off. They will be punished most of all.

a widow's offering

41 Jesus was sitting in the temple near the offering box and watching people put in their gifts. He noticed that many rich people were giving a lot of money.
42 Finally, a poor widow came up and put in two coins that were worth only a few pennies.
43 Jesus told his disciples to gather around him. Then he said:

I tell you that this poor widow has put in more than all the others.
44 Everyone else gave what they didn't need. But she is very poor and gave everything she had. Now she doesn't have a penny to live on.

12:36 right side: *The place of power and honour.*
12:37 David...his son: *See the note at 10:47.*

the temple will be destroyed

13

1As Jesus was leaving the temple, one of his disciples said to him, 'Teacher, look at these beautiful
stones and wonderful buildings!'
2Jesus replied, 'Do you see these huge buildings? They will
certainly be torn down! Not one stone will be left in place.'

warning about trouble

3Later, as Jesus was sitting on the Mount of Olives across
from the temple, Peter, James, John, and Andrew came to
him in private. 4They asked, 'When will these things happen?
What will be the sign that they are about to take place?'
5Jesus answered:

Watch out and don't let anyone fool you! 6Many will
come and claim to be me. They will use my name and fool
many people.
7When you hear about wars and threats of wars, don't
be afraid. These things will have to happen first, but that
isn't the end. 8Nations and kingdoms will go to war against
each other. There will be earthquakes in many places, and
people will starve to death. But this is just the beginning
of troubles.
9Be on your guard! You will be taken to courts and
beaten with whips in their meeting places. And because of
me, you will have to stand before rulers and kings to tell
about your faith. 10But before the end comes, the good
news must be preached to all nations.
11When you are arrested, don't worry about what you
will say. You will be given the right words when the time
comes. But you will not really be the ones speaking. Your
words will come from the Holy Spirit.
12Brothers and sisters will betray each other and have
each other put to death. Parents will betray their own chil-

dren, and children will turn against their parents and have them killed. 13Everyone will hate you because of me. But if you keep on being faithful right to the end, you will be saved.

the Horrible Thing

Jesus continued:

14Some day you will see that 'Horrible Thing' where it should not be. Everyone who reads this must try to understand! If you are living in Judea at that time, run to the mountains. 15If you are on the roof of your house, don't go inside to get anything. 16If you are out in the field, don't go back for your coat. 17It will be an awful time for women who are expecting babies or nursing young children. 18Pray that it won't happen in winter. 19This will be the worst time of suffering since God created the world, and nothing this terrible will ever happen again. 20If the Lord doesn't make the time shorter, no one will be left alive. But because of his chosen and special ones, he will make the time shorter.

21If someone should say, 'Here is the Messiah!' or 'There he is!' don't believe it. 22False messiahs and false prophets will come and perform miracles and signs. They will even try to fool God's chosen ones. 23But be on your guard! That's why I am telling you these things now.

when the Son of Man appears

Jesus continued:

24In those days, straight after that time of suffering,

13:14 where it should not be: *Probably the holy place in the temple.*
13:15 roof: *See the note at 2:4.*
13:18 in winter: *In Palestine the winters are cold and rainy and make travel difficult.*

'The sun will become dark,
and the moon will no longer shine.
25The stars will fall,
and the powers in the sky will be shaken.'

26Then the Son of Man will be seen coming in the
clouds with great power and glory. 27He will send his
angels to gather his chosen ones from all over the earth.

a lesson from a fig tree

Jesus continued:

28Learn a lesson from a fig tree. When its branches
sprout and start putting out leaves, you know summer is
near. 29So when you see all these things happening, you
will know that the time has almost come. 30You can be
sure that some of the people of this generation will still be
alive when all this happens. 31The sky and the earth will
not last for ever, but my words will.

no one knows the day or time

Jesus continued:

32No one knows the day or the time. The angels in
heaven don't know, and the Son himself doesn't know.
Only the Father knows. 33So watch out and be ready! You
don't know when the time will come. 34It is like what happens when a man goes away for a while and places his ser-
vants in charge of everything. He tells each of them what
to do, and he orders the guard to keep alert. 35So be alert!
You don't know when the master of the house will come

13:25 the powers in the sky: *In ancient times people thought that the stars were spiritual powers.*

back. It could be in the evening or at midnight or before dawn or in the morning. 36But if he comes suddenly, don't let him find you asleep. 37I tell everyone just what I have told you. Be alert!

a plot to kill Jesus

14 It was now two days before Passover and the Festival of Thin Bread. The chief priests and the teachers of the Law of Moses were secretly planning to have Jesus arrested and put to death. 2They were saying, 'We must not do it during the festival, because the people will riot.'

at Bethany

3Jesus was eating in Bethany at the home of Simon, who once had leprosy, when a woman came in with a very expensive bottle of sweet-smelling perfume. After breaking it open, she poured the perfume on Jesus' head. 4This made some of the guests angry, and they complained, 'Why such a waste? 5We could have sold this perfume for more than three hundred silver coins and given the money to the poor!' So they started saying cruel things to the woman.

6But Jesus said:

Leave her alone! Why are you bothering her? She has done a beautiful thing for me. 7You will always have the poor with you. And whenever you want to, you can give to them. But you won't always have me here with you. 8She has done all she could by pouring perfume on my body to prepare it for burial. 9You may be sure that wherever the good news is told all over the world, people will remember what she has done. And they will tell others.

14:3 leprosy: *In biblical times the word 'leprosy' was used for many different skin diseases.*

Judas and the chief priests

[10]Judas Iscariot was one of the twelve disciples. He went to the chief priests and offered to help them arrest Jesus. [11]They were glad to hear this, and they promised to pay him. So Judas started looking for a good chance to betray Jesus.

Jesus eats with his disciples

[12]It was the first day of the Festival of Thin Bread, and the Passover lambs were being killed. Jesus' disciples asked him, 'Where do you want us to prepare the Passover meal?'

[13]Jesus said to two of the disciples, 'Go into the city, where you will meet a man carrying a jar of water. Follow him, [14]and when he goes into a house, say to the owner, "Our teacher wants to know if you have a room where he can eat the Passover meal with his disciples." [15]The owner will take you upstairs and show you a large room furnished and ready for you to use. Prepare the meal there.'

'wo disciples went into the city and found everything just as Jesus had told them. So they prepared the Passover meal.

[17–18]While Jesus and the twelve disciples were eating together that evening, he said, 'The one who will betray me is now eating with me.'

[19]This made the disciples sad, and one after another they said to Jesus, 'Surely you don't mean me!'

[20]He answered, 'It is one of you twelve men who is eating from this dish with me. [21] The Son of Man will die, just as the Scriptures say. But it is going to be terrible for the one who betrays me. That man would be better off if he had never been born.'

14:10 Iscariot: *See the note at 3:19.*
14:13 a man carrying a jar of water: *A male slave carrying water could mean that the family was rich.*

the Lord's supper

22During the meal Jesus took some bread in his hands. He
blessed the bread and broke it. Then he gave it to his disciples and said, 'Take this. It is my body.'
23Jesus picked up a cup of wine and gave thanks to God.
He gave it to his disciples, and said, 'Drink it!' So they all
drank some. 24Then he said, 'This is my blood, which is
poured out for many people, and with it God makes his agreement. 25From now on I will not drink any wine, until I drink new
wine in God's kingdom.' 26Then they sang a hymn and went
out to the Mount of Olives.

Peter's promise

27Jesus said to his disciples, 'All of you will reject me, as the
Scriptures say,

"I will strike down the shepherd,
and the sheep will be scattered."

28But after I am raised to life, I will go ahead of you to Galilee.'
29Peter spoke up, 'Even if all the others reject you, I never
will!'
30Jesus replied, 'This very night before a cock crows twice,
you will say three times that you don't know me.'
31But Peter was so sure of himself that he said, 'Even if I
have to die with you, I will never say that I don't know you!'
All the others said the same thing.

Jesus prays

32Jesus went with his disciples to a place called
Gethsemane, and he told them, 'Sit here while I pray.'
33Jesus took along Peter, James, and John. He was sad

and troubled and 34told them, 'I am so sad that I feel as if I am dying. Stay here and keep awake with me.'

35–36Jesus walked on a little way. Then he knelt down on the ground and prayed, 'Father, if it is possible, don't let this happen to me! Father, you can do anything. Don't make me suffer by making me drink from this cup. But do what you want, and not what I want.'

37When Jesus came back and found the disciples sleeping, he said to Simon Peter, 'Are you asleep? Can't you stay awake for just one hour? 38Stay awake and pray that you won't be tested. You want to do what is right, but you are weak.'

39Jesus went back and prayed the same prayer. 40But when he returned to the disciples, he found them sleeping again. They simply could not keep their eyes open, and they did not know what to say.

41When Jesus returned to the disciples the third time, he said, 'Are you still sleeping and resting? Enough of that! The time has come for the Son of Man to be handed over to sinners. 42Get up! Let's go. The one who will betray me is already here.'

Jesus is arrested

43Jesus was still speaking, when Judas the betrayer came up. He was one of the twelve disciples, and a mob of men armed with swords and clubs were with him. They had been sent by the chief priests, the nation's leaders, and the teachers of the Law of Moses. 44Judas had told them beforehand, 'Arrest the man I greet with a kiss. Tie him up tight and lead him away.'

14:35–36 by making me drink from this cup: *See the note at 10:38.*
14:44 greet with a kiss: *It was the custom for people to greet each other with a kiss on the cheek.*

45Judas walked right up to Jesus and said, 'Teacher!' Then
Judas kissed him, 46and the men grabbed Jesus and arrested
him.

47Someone standing there pulled out a sword. He struck
the servant of the high priest and cut off his ear.

48Jesus said to the mob, 'Why do you come with swords
and clubs to arrest me like a criminal? 49Day after day I was
with you and taught in the temple, and you didn't arrest me.
But what the Scriptures say must come true.'

50All Jesus' disciples ran off and left him. 51One of them
was a young man who was wearing only a linen cloth. And
when the men grabbed him, 52he left the cloth behind and ran
away naked.

Jesus is questioned by the council

53Jesus was led off to the high priest. Then the chief
priests, the nation's leaders, and the teachers of the Law of
Moses all met together. 54Peter had followed at a distance.
And when he reached the courtyard of the high priest's
house, he sat down with the guards to warm himself beside
a fire.

55The chief priests and the whole council tried to find
someone to accuse Jesus of a crime, so they could put him
to death. But they could not find anyone to accuse him.
56Many people did tell lies against Jesus, but they did not
agree on what they said. 57Finally, some men stood up and
lied about him. They said, 58'We heard him say he would tear
down this temple that we built. He also claimed that in three
days he would build another one without any help.' 59But even
then they did not agree on what they said.

60The high priest stood up in the council and asked Jesus,
'Why don't you say something in your own defence? Don't you
hear the charges they are making against you?' 61But Jesus
kept quiet and did not say a word. The high priest asked him

another question, 'Are you the Messiah, the Son of the glorious God?'

62'Yes, I am!' Jesus answered.

> 'Soon you will see the Son of Man
> sitting at the right side of God All-Powerful,
> and coming with the clouds of heaven.'

63At once the high priest ripped his robe apart and shouted, 'Why do we need more witnesses? 64You heard him claim to be God! What is your decision?' They all agreed that he should be put to death.

65Some of the people started spitting on Jesus. They blindfolded him, hit him with their fists, and said, 'Tell us who hit you!' Then the guards took charge of Jesus and beat him.

Peter says he doesn't know Jesus

66While Peter was still in the courtyard, a servant girl of the high priest came up 67and saw Peter warming himself by the fire. She stared at him and said, 'You were with Jesus from Nazareth!'

68Peter replied, 'That isn't true! I don't know what you're talking about. I don't have any idea what you mean.' He went out to the gate, and a cock crowed.

69The servant girl saw Peter again and said to the people standing there, 'This man is one of them!'

70'No, I'm not!' Peter replied.

A little while later some of the people said to Peter, 'You certainly are one of them. You're a Galilean!'

71This time Peter began to curse and swear, 'I don't even know the man you're talking about!'

14:61 Son of the glorious God: *'Son of God' was one of the titles used for the kings of Israel.*

14:62 right side: *See the note at 12:36.*

[72]Straight away the cock crowed a second time. Then Peter remembered that Jesus had told him, 'Before a cock crows twice, you will say three times that you don't know me.' So Peter started crying.

Pilate questions Jesus

15 Early the next morning the chief priests, the nation's leaders, and the teachers of the Law of Moses met together with the whole Jewish council. They tied up Jesus and led him off to Pilate.

[2]He asked Jesus, 'Are you the king of the Jews?'

'Those are your words,' Jesus answered.

[3]The chief priests brought many charges against Jesus. [4]Then Pilate questioned him again, 'Don't you have anything to say? Don't you hear what crimes they say you have done?' [5]But Jesus did not answer, and Pilate was amazed.

the death sentence

[6]During Passover, Pilate always freed one prisoner chosen by the people. [7]And at that time there was a prisoner named Barabbas. He and some others had been arrested for murder during a riot. [8]The crowd now came and asked Pilate to set a prisoner free, just as he usually did. [9]Pilate asked them, 'Do you want me to free the king of the Jews?' [10]Pilate knew that the chief priests had brought Jesus to him because they were jealous.

[11]But the chief priests told the crowd to ask Pilate to free Barabbas.

[12]Then Pilate asked the crowd, 'What do you want me to do with this man you say is the king of the Jews?

[13]They yelled, 'Nail him to a cross!'

[14]Pilate asked, 'But what crime has he done?'

'Nail him to a cross!' they yelled even louder.

[15]Pilate wanted to please the crowd. So he set Barabbas

free. Then he ordered his soldiers to beat Jesus with a whip and nail him to a cross.

soldiers make fun of Jesus

16The soldiers led Jesus inside the courtyard of the fortress and called together the rest of the troops. 17They put a purple robe on him, and on his head they placed a crown that they had made out of thorn branches. 18They made fun of Jesus and shouted, 'Hey, you king of the Jews!' 19Then they beat him on the head with a stick. They spat on him and knelt down and pretended to worship him.

20When the soldiers had finished making fun of Jesus, they took off the purple robe. They put his own clothes back on him and led him off to be nailed to a cross. 21Simon from Cyrene happened to be coming in from a farm, and they forced him to carry Jesus' cross. Simon was the father of Alexander and Rufus.

Jesus is nailed to a cross

22The soldiers took Jesus to Golgotha, which means 'Place of a Skull'. 23There they gave him some wine mixed with a drug to ease the pain, but he refused to drink it.

24They nailed Jesus to a cross and gambled to see who would get his clothes. 25It was about nine o'clock in the morning when they nailed him to the cross. 26On it was a sign that told why he was nailed there. It read, 'This is the King of the Jews.' 27–28The soldiers also nailed two criminals on crosses, one to the right of Jesus and the other to his left.

15:16 fortress: *The place where the Roman governor stayed. It was probably at Herod's palace west of Jerusalem, though it may have been Fortress Antonia, north of the temple, where the Roman troops were stationed.*

15:17 purple robe: *This was probably a Roman soldier's robe.*

15:22 Place of a Skull: *The place was probably given this name because it was near a large rock in the shape of a human skull.*

29People who passed by said terrible things about Jesus.
They shook their heads and shouted, 'Ha! So you're the one
who claimed you could tear down the temple and build it
again in three days. 30Save yourself and come down from the
cross!'
31The chief priests and the teachers of the Law of Moses
also made fun of Jesus. They said to each other, 'He saved
others, but he can't save himself. 32If he is the Messiah, the
king of Israel, let him come down from the cross! Then we will
see and believe.' The two criminals also said cruel things to
Jesus.

the death of Jesus

33About midday the sky turned dark and stayed that way until
around three o'clock. 34Then about that time Jesus shouted,
'Eloi, Eloi, lema sabachthani?' which means, 'My God, my
God, why have you deserted me?'
35Some of the people standing there heard Jesus and
said, 'He is calling for Elijah.' 36One of them ran and grabbed
a sponge. After he had soaked it in wine, he put it on a stick
and held it up to Jesus. He said, 'Let's wait and see if Elijah
will come and take him down!' 37Jesus shouted and then
died.
38At once the curtain in the temple tore in two from top to
bottom.
39A Roman army officer was standing in front of Jesus.
When the officer saw how Jesus died, he said, 'This man
really was the Son of God!'

15:34 Eloi ... sabachthani: *These words are in Aramaic, a language spoken in Palestine during the time of Jesus.*

15:35 Elijah: *The name 'Elijah' sounds something like 'Eloi', which means 'my God'.*

15:36 see if Elijah will come: *See the note at 6:15.*

15:38 curtain in the temple: *There were two curtains in the temple. One was at the entrance, and the other separated the holy place from the most holy place that the Jewish people thought of as God's home on earth. The second curtain is probably the one which is meant.*

40–41Some women were looking on from a distance. They
had come with Jesus to Jerusalem. But even before this they
had been his followers and had helped him while he was in
Galilee. Mary Magdalene and Mary the mother of the younger
James and of Joseph were two of these women. Salome was
also one of them.

Jesus is buried

42It was now the evening before the Sabbath, and the Jewish
people were getting ready for that sacred day. 43A man named
Joseph from Arimathea was brave enough to ask Pilate for the
body of Jesus. Joseph was a highly respected member of the
Jewish council, and he was also waiting for God's kingdom to
come.
44Pilate was surprised to hear that Jesus was already
dead, and he called in the army officer to find out if Jesus had
been dead very long. 45After the officer told him, Pilate let
Joseph have Jesus' body.
46Joseph bought a linen cloth and took the body down from
the cross. He had it wrapped in the cloth, and he put it in a
tomb that had been cut into solid rock. Then he rolled a big
stone against the entrance to the tomb.
47Mary Magdalene and Mary the mother of Joseph were
watching and saw where the body was placed.

Jesus is alive

16

After the Sabbath, Mary Magdalene, Salome, and
Mary the mother of James bought some spices to
put on Jesus' body. 2Very early on Sunday morning,
just as the sun was coming up, they went to the tomb. 3On
their way, they were asking one another, 'Who will roll the
stone away from the entrance for us?' 4But when they looked,
they saw that the stone had already been rolled away. And it
was a huge stone!

[5]The women went into the tomb, and on the right side they saw a young man in a white robe sitting there. They were alarmed.

[6]The man said, 'Don't be alarmed! You are looking for Jesus from Nazareth, who was nailed to a cross. God has raised him to life, and he isn't here. You can see the place where they put his body. [7]Now go and tell his disciples, and especially Peter, that he will go ahead of you to Galilee. You will see him there, just as he told you.'

[8]When the women ran from the tomb, they were confused and shaking all over. They were too afraid to tell anyone what had happened.

One old ending to Mark's Gospel

Jesus appears to his followers

Jesus appears to Mary Magdalene

[9]Very early on the first day of the week, after Jesus had risen to life, he appeared to Mary Magdalene. Earlier he had forced seven demons out of her. [10]She left and told his friends, who were crying and mourning. [11]Even though they heard that Jesus was alive and that Mary had seen him, they would not believe it.

Jesus appears to two disciples

[12]Later, Jesus appeared in another form to two disciples, as they were on their way out of the city. [13]But when these disciples told what had happened, the others would not believe.

what Jesus' followers must do

[14]Afterwards, Jesus appeared to his eleven disciples as they

were eating. He scolded them because they were too stubborn to believe the ones who had seen him after he had been raised to life. 15Then he told them:

> Go and preach the good news to everyone in the world.
> 16Anyone who believes me and is baptized will be saved.
> But anyone who refuses to believe me will be condemned.
> 17Everyone who believes me will be able to do wonderful
> things. By using my name they will force out demons, and
> they will speak new languages. 18They will handle snakes
> and will drink poison and not be hurt. They will also heal
> sick people by placing their hands on them.

Jesus returns to heaven

19After the Lord Jesus had said these things to the disciples,
he was taken back up to heaven where he sat down at the
right side of God. 20Then the disciples left and preached
everywhere. The Lord was with them, and the miracles they
performed proved that their message was true.

Another old ending to Mark's gospel

9–10The women quickly told Peter and his friends what had happened. Later, Jesus sent the disciples to the east and to the west with his sacred and everlasting message of how people can be saved for ever.

conclusion

So what do you make of Mark, the first written 'Gospel' about Jesus?

I am sure you noticed the breathless haste with which he writes (his account is full of phrases like 'straight away', 'at once'). You will have noticed his short graphic paragraphs, each emphasizing some critical word or action of Jesus, which challenge the reader to make up his or her mind and decide. You will have seen how Mark lays down his own convictions in the very first verse, calling Jesus Christ the Son of God. His account shows why he was driven to that conclusion. He concludes with three major themes.

The death of Jesus. Did you notice that brief comment in 15:38 immediately after the account of the death of Jesus – and before the officer in charge of the execution had exclaimed, "This man really was the Son of God!'? Mark records that the curtain of the temple was torn in two from top to bottom. That great curtain kept people out of the inner part of the temple where God's presence could be encountered. Nobody ever went in there except the High Priest to offer sacrifice once a year. Mark sees the death of Jesus as the supreme sacrifice. It tears apart that 'veil of unknowing' which separates humanity from God. Access is open to all – even for the officer who killed him.

The resurrection of Jesus. Though utterly unexpected, the resurrection is solid history. Mark records here a number of people who could bear testimony to it, men and women alike (16:1, 12–14). Although they were, naturally, overcome with fear (verse 8) and slow to credit it at first (verse 11), once they were convinced that Jesus was alive, they 'left and preached everywhere' (verse 20). This was too good, too important, to keep to themselves.

The challenge of Jesus. Mark is very clear about this. Jesus' clear command was to 'go and preach the good news to everyone in the world' (16:15). Maybe some of your Christian friends have been doing this to you! Mark insists that we cannot escape the challenge of responding to Jesus. He puts it with great bluntness: 'Anyone who believes and is baptized will be saved. But anyone who refuses to believe me will be condemned' (verse 16). He could not have put it more plainly than that. How about you? Where do you stand?

You may feel, like the man that Mark describes in chapter 9, 'I do have faith! Please help me to have even more' (9:24). Well, tell the Lord that. It is a prayer to which he will always respond. And you can go on your way confident that whoever believes and is baptized will be saved! Don't keep it to yourself. Go, like the disciples in these final verses of the Gospel, and tell someone else – initially, someone who can give you a bit of help in the early days of following Jesus.

Michael Green

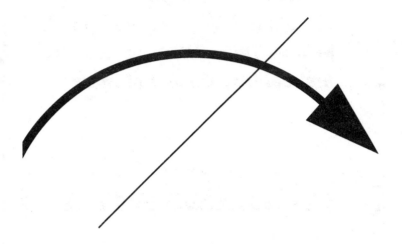

And if you have not already done so, why not read chapter 6, 'Rumours of life', which will help explain where to go from here.

[postscript]

michael green

STRANGE INTELLIGENCE

inter-varsity press

INTER-VARSITY PRESS
38 De Montfort Street, Leicester LE1 7GP, England

The material by Michael Green has been adapted from his book *Critical Choices* (IVP, 1995).
Thanks to Rupert Edwards and his friends on the OICCU mission committee 1996–7 for their help on this book.

First published under the title Strange Intelligence *in a limited edition in 1996*

This edition published 1997

British Library Cataloguing in Publication Data
A catalogue record for this book is available from the British Library.

ISBN 0–85111–192–0

Set in Franklin Gothic
Typeset in Great Britain by Avocet Typeset, Brill, Aylesbury, Bucks.
Printed in Great Britain by The Guernsey Press Co. Ltd., Guernsey, Channel Islands

Inter-Varsity Press is the book-publishing division of the Universities and Colleges Christian Fellowship (formerly the Inter-Varsity Fellowship), a student movement linking Christian Unions in universities and colleges throughout the United Kingdom and the Republic of Ireland, and a member movement of the International Fellowship of Evangelical Students. For information about local and national activities write to UCCF, 38 De Montfort Street, Leicester LE1 7GP.

CONTENTS

1 familiar voices

If you browse through the *X Files* T-shirts in your local mall you'll find three well-known captions. They evoke the essence of some of the problems we face when asking the really big questions about life.

'The truth is out there' – yet agents Scully and Mulder find that it is always just out of their grasp. If it is there, it can't be located. 'I want to believe' – but Scully's overt scepticism always holds her back. 'Trust no-one' – look for answers but trust only yourself to find them.

These sentiments can be found in the (conflicting) thoughts of many academics:

'The human race must realise how insignificant it is. We are just a bit of slime on a planet belonging to one sun!'
(*Dr Peter Atkins in the* Sunday Telegraph, *7 April 1996*)

'Intelligent life on a planet comes of age when it first works out the reason for its own existence.'
(*Richard Dawkins,* The Selfish Gene)

'Either the moral law is valid because it emanates from God's will or its validity is independent from God. If the latter is the case, then God is not the ultimate moral authority.'
(*Joseph Raz,* The Morality of Freedom)

'If God exists, then arguments about him are arguments about the cosmos and of cosmic importance, but if he does not, they are about nothing. In that case, the important questions must be about human beings, and why, for instance, they ever believed God existed.'
(*Bernard Williams,* Ethics and the Limits of Philosophy)

'Different religions are in conflict ... the miracle reports of any one religion are implicitly or in effect contradicted by the miracle reports of many other religions: it is as if the law court were presented with, say, twenty witnesses, each of which was denounced as a liar by the other nineteen.'
(J. L. Mackie, The Miracle of Theism)

The Universe is progressing from a state of extremely high order to a state of increasing disorder, and, according to Professor Roger Penrose, the amount of order required at the *beginning*, for a universe which looks like ours *today*, *i.e.* with galaxies and life, is phenomenal:

'This now tells us how precise the Creator's aim must have been: namely to an accuracy of

one part in $10^{10^{123}}$

This is an extraordinary figure. One could not possibly *write the number down* in full ... it would be "1" followed by 10^{123} successive "0"s! Even if we were to write a "0" on each separate proton and on each separate

neutron in the entire universe ... we should fall far short of writing down the figure needed.'

(*Roger Penrose,* The Emperor's New Mind)

'The experience of so many men in their moments of religious vision corroborates what nature and history show to be quite likely – that there is a God who made and sustains the universe.'

(*Richard Swinburne,* The Existence of God)

'Just a bit of slime?' When it comes to the big questions, there are a multitude of claims and beliefs to chose from. Many of them are espoused by decent, reasonable people. Can we choose between them? Or are we paralysed by choice? Frozen into a kind of agnostic coma? After all, why is your choice any better than mine? The truth may be out there ... but it can't be located. A part of me may even want to believe that the big questions can be answered ... but why should I trust anyone else's answers? I'll work out my own, thanks. That is ... when I get the time.

Our habitat is frantic. We are surrounded by innumerable choices. What with study or employment (or McJobs!), friends to see, parties, pubs and clubs, work and leisure, there never seems enough time to sort them all out. As a result we tend to go through life paying attention to the immediate pressures upon us, but content to stack the critical issues away to be handled if and when there is time. This book is about those critical issues.

There is a powerful story told by Jorge Borges in *The Library of Babel.* He sees the universe as a gigantic library. At first you are thrilled as you grasp the keys which allow you entry to the library. You are thrilled as you move along gallery after gallery of books. There is no problem in the world which does not have a solution somewhere on those shelves. But before long you give up in despair. There is far too much to know, too many choices to be made. Life is not long enough.

You feel you know more and more about less and less. You came in looking for truth, and you end up confused and disappointed and, like the librarian in the story, hoping against hope that there must be on some shelf a book that makes sense of all the others, and better still, a man 'analogous to God' as Borges puts it, who can explain it all. But the man in the story dies in despair because he never finds that book or meets the person who could make sense of it all.

That is what happens if we shut God out of our lives. There is a book which makes sense of the whole library of life, and it is the world's best seller. There is a man 'analogous to God' who can explain it all, and we date our era by him. He is not hiding from us in the recesses of the library. He has come to meet us.

That is what happened at the first Christmas. But we turn our backs on him, do we not? We keep out of his way because he sees right through us. It is uncomfortable. We want to do away with him.

That is what happened at the crucifixion. But we can't get rid of him. He comes to life again.

That is what happened on the first Easter Day. Indeed, he longs to come into our lives, clean them up, and become the integrating force in our personalities and our society.

That is what happened to the first disciples: it has been happening ever since.

Yes, in the midst of a baffling plethora of choices for our own activities and lifestyle, there is a book which makes sense of it all, and there is a man who can be our guide. I have found this to be both true and deeply fulfilling; that is why I have written this book. But I want readers to make up their own minds. We never take anything on board based on someone else's say-so. Therefore you will not find in these pages a heavy treatise on Christian dogma. It deals with the practical issues we all have to face: our identity, our human predicament, our delusions. It looks at our longing for freedom, our strains and stresses, our hunger for love and rela-

tionships, and wonders whether these areas of universal human experience point us to the book and the 'man analogous to God' who can make sense of it all. If so, then the most fundamental of all human characteristics must come into play. We must choose. And of all choices we shall ever make, this could be the most critical. Shall we, or shall we not, follow that man analogous to God?

2

some sneaking suspicions

are there footprints in the sand?

Richard Dawkins holds that the Starbridge Chair in Theology and Natural Science at Cambridge is a total waste of money. Why? Theology is, in his view, a non-subject, unworthy of serious academic attention. Is he right?

The celebrated astronomer Carl Sagan opened his television series *Cosmos* with the dogmatic claim, 'The cosmos is all there is or ever was, or ever will be.' But was he right?

Sagan himself was not so sure as he appeared. In his later writings he found himself moving towards the conviction that there must be some mysterious divine force behind the cosmos itself. Which of us has not been struck by the splendour of the Milky Way on a frosty night, and marvelled at its beauty and immensity? 'I can see how it might be possible for a man to look upon the earth and be an atheist,' said Abraham Lincoln, 'but I cannot conceive how he can look up into the heavens and say there is no God.'

The trouble is that God is very much out of fashion. And

that counts against him more than any arguments. It is not cool to believe.

There is a fascinating illustration of this point in the first of C. S. Lewis's *Screwtape Letters*. Screwtape, the chief devil, writes to Wormwood, his amateur associate, about the irrelevance of truth:

> Your man has been accustomed ever since he was a boy to have a dozen incompatible philosophies dancing around in his head. He doesn't think of doctrines as true or false, but as outworn or contemporary, conventional or ruthless. Jargon, not argument, is your best ally in keeping him from the church. Don't waste time making him think materialism is true. Make him think it is strong, or stark, or courageous – that is the philosophy of the future. That's the sort of thing he cares about.

Is it not like that with us? God does not seem a plausible hypothesis these days, so we do not bother to give the matter serious consideration. We squeeze all thought of these ultimate concerns from our minds under the tyranny of the urgent.

Maybe it would be a good idea to face the issue. Are we orphans in a land of no tomorrow? Are we merely a grown-up bunch of genes? Or is there more to the world and ourselves? 'In the beginning God created the heavens and the earth,' says the Bible in its opening sentence. That might just be true. If so, it has phenomenal consequences for all of us.

is anyone there?

Well, if God exists, we might reasonably expect him to have left his footprints in the sands of our world. And please note that by 'God' I do not mean the New Age idea of a god which is the cosmos and all that is in it, but no more. No, I mean a

God with a capital 'G', the creator, sustainer and goal of the whole cosmos – but by no means to be equated with it. The God who combines transcendence (over and beyond our world) with immanence (showing his hand within it). What footprints might such a God be expected to leave?

Let's begin with a man who made few pretensions to religious faith when he wrote *A Rumour of Angels*. Peter Berger is a very open-minded and perceptive sociologist. He drew attention to a number of 'signals of transcendence' which we all acknowledge, but which are very hard to explain if there is no God.

One is *order*. All societies have an instinct for order, and it ties in with the order we see in the world around us. 'Human order in some way corresponds to an order which transcends it ... an order man can trust himself and his destiny to,' writes Berger. 'Thus man's ordering propensity implies a transcendent order.' If there is order in the world, how did it get there?

Another is *play*. It suspends, for a moment, our serious 'living towards death' as we experience again the 'deathlessness' of childhood. Play, he suggests, is a very odd thing to find in a world which has no Creator and no goal.

Hope is a third signal of transcendence. It is a universal part of human experience. It continues to the bitter end of our lives. It is like a silver thread, interwoven with our experience at every point, but originating outside of us.

A fourth strand of the transcendent in our experience is what Berger calls the argument from *damnation*. He thinks of situations where our humanity is so outraged by actions like the Holocaust that we think no punishment, even death, is enough for the perpetrators. That is a very interesting phenomenon, if death is the ultimate sanction. Where could the idea have come from?

Fifth, *humour*. What an astonishing thing to find in a world that has no personal Creator! Humour recognizes the imprisonment of the human spirit in the world, and also, for a

moment, liberates it. It gives a sense of proportion which makes our predicament for the moment tolerable.

Those indications that there is Something or Someone beyond could be expanded considerably. I don't propose to do that now. Instead, I would like to ask a question. Just suppose for a moment that the vast majority of humankind across the world and down the ages is right, and there is a God, a supreme source from which all else flows. Go further and imagine yourself to be God. After all, if the actress and author Shirley MacLaine could do that, why not you? What would you do if you wanted to reach out to the human beings you had made in your own likeness, but who did not want to know you?

footprints in the sand?

You might start by creating a marvellous *world*, a world which shouted out the love and skill and power of the Creator. Well, perhaps God has done just that.

Then you might create *people* who are capable of responding to love. People with the dangerous gift of free will, able either to respond to you or reject you. They would have that almost divine capacity for self-determination and free choice. Well, maybe God took the risk and did that too.

You could then go on to instil in the hearts of these people *values* which spoke of God. Values like beauty, goodness, harmony, creativity, speech, truth, love. Wherever they are found, these qualities would point to the Giver; the one who is unutterable beauty, supreme goodness, total harmony, unceasing creativity. They would be the imprint of the God who leaves his footsteps in the sand of our lives. Perhaps God has done that.

You might like the idea of building in a *conscience*, which would approve when these people chose the right way, and would prod them and warn them when they went astray from your will which was their highest good. A conscience which

would persevere however much they tried to stifle it. Could God have done that, too?

You could after that instil a *God-shaped blank* in their lives, a hole which nothing else can fill apart from the living God himself. A space which cries out for satisfaction and fulfilment however much rubbish they crowd into it.

You might then show your hand in the course of *history*. You might ensure that the arrogance of nations and civilizations led inevitably to corruption and fall. You might concentrate on one man, one family, one tribe, one nation which would trust you and obey you, and through them you could in time make yourself known to the world. Did not God do precisely that, with the people of Israel?

Finally, just conceivably, you might *come in person* to their world. You would have to come as one of them, for if you disclosed yourself in all your radiant beauty they would be blinded by the sight. It would be very costly. You would have to love them an awful lot if you were going to shrink yourself down to their level. It would be rather like one of us becoming a rat or a slug – in order really to communicate effectively with such lowly creatures. It would be an almost unthinkable sacrifice. But what if God did that too?

That – no less – is what overwhelmed the first Christians.

> Jesus Christ shared the very nature of God. But he did not consider equality with God something to be held on to. He made himself nothing. He assumed the very nature of a servant. He became one of us. And as he shared our human nature he humbled himself, and became obedient to death – even on a cross. That is why God exalted him to the highest place in the universe, and gave him the name that is above every name that at the name of Jesus every knee should bow, and every tongue confess that Jesus Christ is Lord, to the glory of God the Father.
>
> (*Philippians 2:6–11, my translation*)

Are we alone in the universe? Or are there footsteps in the sand, leading gently to the one who made those imprints, and lived among us, died among us? We have the privilege of making up our minds about where the evidence points. We are free agents. We all have to exercise faith – either the atheist's faith that there is no God, or the believer's faith that there is. It is faith either way. So how does it strike you? Are Carl Sagan and Richard Dawkins right when they claim that the cosmos is all there ever was or is or ever will be? Or have you a sneaking suspicion that they might have missed out on the footprints?

real lives

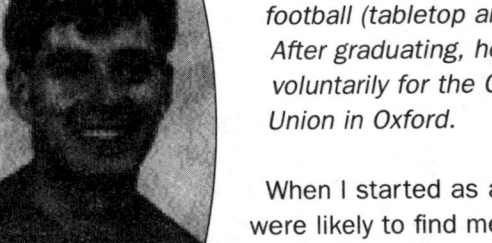

Rob Fuller *read Physics at university, where he played a fair game of football (tabletop and turftop). After graduating, he worked voluntarily for the Christian Union in Oxford.*

When I started as a student, you were likely to find me on the footie pitch or in the pub on a Sunday. Certainly not in church. My interests lay solely in the sphere of wine, women and song (and a bit of work too). While I didn't have a religious upbringing, I did on occasions wonder what it was all about. Yet, as a physicist, I naïvely assumed that only science held the key to the big questions of life.

Coming to college was the first time I met committed Christians of my own age. To my surprise, they were clearly intelligent people who didn't seem particularly gullible. So I

was intrigued and slightly incredulous that they could believe such fairy tales. Especially the scientists. Curiosity got the better of me and I began to investigate, looking perversely, I think, to disprove their beliefs.

One thing that struck me as I looked was the integrity of lifestyle displayed by the Christians. They had better, more real friendships and better attitudes to other people. This is a generalization, but I didn't find the hypocrisy that the media are so keen to expose in the established church.

I spent a year asking questions and found consistently that the Christians did not have a blind faith but coherent and well-thought-out beliefs. I found that my argument that Christianity was contradicted by science did not prove to be valid. Also, their honest analysis of human nature as flawed and self-centred, and the radical solution being found in the cross of Jesus, was compelling. I asked loads of questions, went to hear speakers and I even went to a series of 'enquiry' meetings that discussed the nuts and bolts of Christianity. I discovered that it is entirely consistent with the evidence. As I looked, I found that the real issue was about how I responded to the living person: Jesus Christ. Not whether I believe in some abstract concept of God. Eventually I committed my life to following Jesus.

People responded in a variety of ways. Some were contemptuous and ostracized me. I continue to be disappointed at some people's unwillingness to consider deeper questions. But others were very positive and supportive. Three years down the track, I know it is the most important decision I'll ever make.

3 some nagging doubts

i. who on earth am I?

a number? worthless? wonderful?

In the Museum of Fine Arts at Boston, Massachusetts, there is a remarkable canvas. It was painted by Paul Gauguin, and it poses three of the most penetrating questions it is possible to ask: Where do I come from? Who on earth am I? Where am I going? Needless to say the painter does not offer us any solutions, and neither does anyone else these days. Maybe we are too much into our creature comforts and information highways to ask basic questions like that. Even the philosophers have for the most part given up: they have long tended to confine their enquiries to linguistic analysis. Maybe it is too threatening to face up to the really big questions.

Nevertheless, the big questions do haunt all of us sometimes, perhaps when we lie awake at night. They are questions to which atheism has no answer. And they will not go away. A fourteen-year-old put it like this:

Why am I here? What have I done? Why was I born? Who cares about me? I am me. I must suffer because I am me. Why do we live? For love, for happiness? Why should I not commit suicide? I hate this world. I hate my parents and my home – though why, I do not know. I searched for truth, but I only found uncertainty. I was thwarted in my search for love. Where can I find happiness? I do not know. Perhaps I shall never know.

Dietrich Bonhoeffer, celebrated professor and patriot, had similar heart-searchings as he lay in a Nazi prison before his execution for plotting Hitler's assassination:

Who am I? This or the other? Am I one person today and another tomorrow? Am I both at once? They mock me, these lonely questions of mine.

But because he was a Christian, he could dare to end his reflections: 'Whatever I am, you know, God, that I am yours.'

More recently Bernard Levin, the journalist, asked poignantly,

To put it bluntly, have I time to discover why I was born before I die? ... I have not managed to answer that question yet, and however many years I have before me they are certainly not as many as there are behind. There is an obvious danger in leaving it too late ... Why do I have to know why I was born? Because, of course, I am unable to believe it was an accident, and if it wasn't one, it must have a meaning.

That problem of personal identity is both pressing and perplexing these days. There is biological engineering. There is massive manipulation through advertising. There is the pressure of fashion, the peer group, sexual politics. Not to mention the government and the job market. But in the

midst of all this, who am I?

Am I just a number? That is what the prisoners in Auschwitz were. That is what I am to British Telecom. Michael Green does not exist as far as they are concerned. But number EM 1524 4886 Q 072 GY does!

Am I just a combination of chemicals in suspension? Totally determined by the matter of which I am composed? That is what behaviourist philosophers want me to believe. I have just one sneaking problem about that. Who is the 'I' who has made this shattering discovery? And what is the force of the argument that I am totally determined? Is it supposed to have a truth value? How come? For it, too, is totally determined – by the molecules of the brain which makes the claim! All determinist arguments, which trash human dignity, are actually self-defeating. We are supposed to agree with them because they are put forward as true. But on determinist grounds there is no truth: I accept the argument or reject it according to the disposition of my mental molecules. And they are all predetermined! No, that will not do as an explanation of who I am.

Am I simply worthless? A lot of people feel that way today. Great numbers have been abused in childhood. Even more have never known what it is to be truly loved without strings attached. Almost half the marriages in the West today end in divorce, and recent research has revealed the obvious – that it is the children who suffer in a multitude of ways, but most of all in a sense of worthlessness. Nobody cares about me. It wouldn't matter if I died – and that is why an increasing number of under twenty-fives, especially males, contemplate suicide, and many carry it out, and also why a staggering number of female students suffer from eating disorders. After all, my parents don't want me. My girlfriend or boyfriend drops me. And if I am lucky enough to get a job, it will probably not suit my education and personality. Furthermore, for the first time for generations, young adults can expect to be much worse off than their parents.

Circumstances conspire to persuade us that we are not worth a great deal. Yet our instincts tell us this is false. Hence the confusion, anger and despair so common today among young people.

Or am I wonderful? There are the optimists who say the world is getting better all the time, and that we had better learn to play the role of God. You have to live a sheltered life to believe that these days. Alex Comfort predicted that in a hundred years a world population of 15 billion would each have three homes, two cars, and (rather oddly) one submarine, *given reasonable behaviour*! Ah, there's the rub. We do not seem to be capable of reasonable behaviour. There is a perverse twist in human nature. The world is not a better place: it is a wicked place. What generation has seen genocide like Bosnia, Ruanda or Sudan? What century has witnessed such terrorism, such inner-city decay, such famine, such crime? No, I am not so wonderful. Neither are you! We all have a dark side.

a different perspective

If you and I are simply a bunch of atoms in suspension, it is not surprising that we are perplexed about our identity. Why not try the other option? What if you are the product of a living, personal God, the loving source of all there is? He has created this world of ours out of his sheer love. He made us, and we are uniquely special to him. He is so committed to us that although we turn our backs on him, he comes to find us – even to die for us. Beat that if you can!

That is the God I know and love and worship. Indeed, for my money, only such a God is worthy of worship. His love, his splendour, his incredible humility bring me to my knees. In the light of that origin, that price tag, that possibility of relationship and return, then I know who I am, where I came from, and where I am going. I do not come from plankton soup, subsist for a few years as a gene-carrier, and then go

out like a candle. No, I came from God. For years I turned my back on him and argued he didn't exist. But I have elected to turn back to God from my alienation and despair. I have found his loving arms the most dependable in all the world. I live this life in company with him. And at the end of the day my destiny is not just extinction but lasting companionship with him. If I risk all, and commit myself to that worldview rather than the materialist and atheist one, it makes a profound difference.

ii. male and female

'I am a lesbian trapped in a man's body'

'I am a lesbian trapped in a man's body,' says Douglas Coupland's anti-hero in his *Generation X*. Questions of gender and sexuality are extremely complex in this postmodern age. What does it mean to be a male or a female today? The gender confusion is immense. It comes over brilliantly in a film which unexpectedly turned into a major hit: *The Crying Game*. Here the female lead turns out to be a man, just as the relationship between her and the terrorist anti-hero gets sexual. But loyalty and tenderness remain, despite his prison sentence. It is a fascinating expression of the current confusion of male and female roles in society – perhaps seen at its most obvious (and yet most fashionable) in the advertising for Calvin Klein's CK One, 'a fragrance for men and women', in which Kate Moss and her gang all look coolly androgynous. Naturally this leads to widespread sexual experimentation, understandable but often full of pain and frustration.

It is becoming rather less opaque for women than for men these days. There is still the injustice of work and pay inequality. There is still the 'glass ceiling' above which it is highly unusual for a woman to rise. And women face the agony of tension between career and home. They spend

years earning degrees and doing professional training: it seems absurd to stop and give it all up. But it seems just as absurd to have a child and then leave it for someone else to raise. Despite the massive advance of the women's movement in the last half-century, the haunting questions remain, 'How am I best to deploy my life? Who on earth am I?'

Currently it is even more difficult for men. The Swinging Sixties changed women but the Nurturing Nineties are changing men. They are expected to be sensitive as well as manly, to cook as well as play sport, to bath the kids and spend time caring for them, and not leave it all to their partners. They are to be strong yet totally rid of male aggression and the overbearing arrogance that has, alas, been so common down countless centuries. And the change is all supposed to happen now, in one generation – a generation, moreover, when the woman may prove to be the better breadwinner as well as homemaker.

Rosalind Miles in *The Independent* newspaper poses the male dilemma well:

> Over the past twenty years, feminism has been redrawing the maps, rewriting the rules and redefining the meaning of things unquestioned for thousands of years. But we have hardly given a thought to the men ... And many men are left feeling like lost boys in this post-patriarchal world where their prerogatives and perks have been blown away.

Where does the male fit in? Well may he ask, 'Who the hell am I?'

That is precisely the question actor and writer Dirk Bogarde faced as his career took off. 'I rather liked it all. There was one wavering doubt, however, just one. Who the hell was I? There was a vast vacuum, and in spite of a house, car, all my family and possessions, I belonged no-

where.' It's a question that demands an answer.

iii. love and sex

the sexologist's revolution

Every hoarding, every TV advert tells us – as if we did not know – that love and sex are the most important things in life. But so often sex disappoints. As all the popular songs recognize, ours is a society where we are free to abandon one another at whim. Sex is a plaything to be used and discarded like a polystyrene cup. And it hurts terribly to begin with – until you get hardened to it, and give up even hoping for the loving tenderness and stability which, in your heart of hearts, you long for.

So, after years of advocating the opposite, the sexologists Masters and Johnson now advocate seeing sex as an expression of self-giving love between two people who intend it to be for life. Terribly unfashionable, but profoundly human. What could be more dehumanizing, more exploitative, than for me to stay with my partner just while she is young, lively and sexy – and then to jettison her for a more up-to-date model when she becomes a little obsolescent? Yet that is what the Brave New World of today regards as normal. It is not normal. It is sick. I see the other sex not as something to be taken advantage of, raped and violated, but rather as *someone* to whom I can give myself in tenderness, intimacy and for keeps. In our hearts we all long for love like this. The trouble is, it is so difficult. That is where God's help comes in – but more of that anon.

The hunger for a relationship that makes sense in our wasteland of a world comes through powerfully in Sting's song 'If I ever lose my faith in you'. If personal relationship disintegrates, we are indeed lost.

You could say I lost my faith in science and progress
You could say I lost my belief in Holy Church
You could say I lost my sense of direction
You could say all this and worse, but
If I ever lose my faith in you
There'd be nothing left for me to do.
Some would say I was a lost man in a lost world.

I never saw no miracle of science
That didn't go from a blessing to a curse
I never saw no military solution
That didn't always end up as something worse, but
Let me say this first
If I ever lose my faith in you,
There'd be nothing left for me to do.

Powerful, is it not? Distrust of institutions. Trust in just one special friend. And the fear that the friend may desert you, and leave you with nothing but aloneness.

aloneness

I use the term 'aloneness' rather than 'loneliness' because what I am talking about is true of busy people, popular people, successful people and not just those who are psychologically oriented towards solitude.

The celebrated painter Annigoni was once asked what picture he would most like to be remembered by. 'Solitude' was his reply. He painted no fewer than twelve canvases about it. He said, 'The whole conviction of my life rests upon the belief that loneliness, far from being a rare and curious phenomenon peculiar to myself and a few solitary men, is the central and inevitable fact of human existence.'

In her remarkably perceptive book *A Generation Alone*, Janet Bernardi compares her fellow-members of Generation X to random molecules bumping into other molecules. She

goes on to make the important distinction between loneliness, which is a state of emptiness, and aloneness, where the life may be full of activities but lacks the support of family and friends. It encompasses, she says, a basic distrust of people and a fear of being hurt. It is a survival technique and it comes across as independence. For a great number of people in their twenties today that is their overwhelming perception of life. Aloneness.

That is why we try to fill our lives with as many material toys and pleasures as possible. Especially sex.

the misunderstanding of love

'One sentence will suffice for modern man,' said Albert Camus. 'He fornicated and he read the newspapers.'

If ever there was a society in total confusion about love and sexuality, it is ours. Love is undoubtedly our top priority, but we are not at all sure what it is. We used to locate it in happy families, but they seem to be almost a thing of the past. We used to look for it in friendship, but these days friendship without sexuality is considered an aberration. A man can hardly have another man in for a cup of tea in private without being denounced as a homosexual. Even academic interviews are often conducted with the door open for fear of accusations of sexual harassment. Something has gone seriously wrong. That is obvious.

There has been such an erosion of general morality during the past half-century that love in the full-blooded sense, embracing not only sexuality but a sense of partnership, companionship, fidelity, trust, self-giving, respect and consistency, has almost vanished. Instead, selfishness has replaced altruism, hedonism has replaced self-sacrifice, and instant sexual gratification has replaced long-term commitment. No wonder Dudley Moore complains, 'I am always looking for meaningful one night stands.' They don't exist.

Malcolm Muggeridge came to see that 'sex is the mysticism

of materialism, and the only possible religion in a materialistic society'. Aspects of ourselves such as worship, adoration, self-giving, tenderness, feelings, are generally banished from the workplace, but they surface in personal relationships, ideally in sexual intercourse. Since God is out of fashion, it is hardly surprising that sex appears to be the highest good. Sex, so we are told in every movie, every commercial, every book, every magazine, every billboard, is the greatest goal in life. If you aren't having it, you are hopelessly out of date: you haven't lived. The scandal of premarital sex has disappeared: it is replaced by the scandal of virginity. 'There are three really important things in my life,' quipped Woody Allen. 'The first is sex. Somehow the other two don't seem very important now.'

We all know the dangers: a massive rise in teenage pregnancies, sexually transmitted diseases, broken hearts, lies, shattered families, Aids and the rest. It makes no difference. We blindly rush ahead following our hormones.

It is not hard to see where all this has led. It has produced a generation of young adults who are survivors. They have survived the parental selfishness that has either bought them off with presents instead of relationship or given the impression they do not matter, by neglect or divorce. They have survived massive materialist indoctrination through endless hours in front of the TV. And two things have burned deeply into their souls. They know that the material things which bewitched their parents will never satisfy. And despite their initial and thoroughly understandable distrust, they have a deep longing for profound relationships. Has Jesus Christ anything significant to say on this most crucial of all issues? Is Christianity able to help our confusions over love?

the Christian understanding of love

The basic assumption of Christianity is the precise opposite of the hypothesis advanced by Sigmund Freud. He thought that

the idea of a loving God sprang from human love. We thus project our father-image into the sky, call it God, and apply the same emotions to it as we do to our own fathers. So human love is primary and real; love for God is derived and illusory. Christianity, on the contrary, asserts that it is God's love which is primary, and that all human love derives from it and is in some measure (however distorted) a pale reflection of God's love. Far from being the projection of the parent-image into the empty sky, love is the most powerful force in the world precisely because it reflects the fundamental reality about the universe. It comes from God. And God is love. We love, because he first loved us. That is the fundamental Christian conviction on the subject.

love is personal

You cannot have love in a vacuum. The very word involves relationship between persons. To say 'I love' is meaningless. To say 'I love you' is great. And that is what the whole New Testament maintains. 'God so loved the world ... the Son of God loved me ...' We may feel that God could love everyone else, maybe, but he could not love me. Well, Jesus came to show that God does love every one of us.

It comes down to this. You and I don't have to look for God. God is looking for us. He faces us with the person of Jesus and says, in effect, 'There, that is love. Utter self-giving to the utterly undeserving. Will you have it or not?' The love which spun the universe into space has erupted in Jesus. Love confronts us in person and looks for a response. The crucial issue is, 'What do you make of Jesus?' not 'Does God exist?' That is the wrong way to formulate the question. It leaves comfortable room for argument and evasion. But the living God is no 'It' to be analysed and argued about. God is the supreme 'I' to be encountered. And encounter us he does in the person of Jesus – not as a proposition to be argued about but as a person to be met. You cannot love a proposition. The

only way to find out for sure is by meeting. All human love is, by its very nature, interpersonal. God's love cannot be less.

love is satisfying

You know how it is when two people fall in love. They are utterly taken up with one another, deeply satisfied. They have begun to taste a new and shared life, and it is wonderful. 'When someone really loves you, that's when your life begins ...'

Unfortunately, it often dies very quickly: sometimes it ripens into marriage. But even so, all human love is incomplete. It points to something beyond itself. It reaches out towards an experience which it does not itself satisfy. Hardly surprising, if the Great Lover is excluded from our lives. Oh, I know we don't picture him as that. He feels like the Great Policeman. His aim, we fear, is to make life respectable and dull, not joyful and satisfying. Well, wherever we got that idea from, it owes nothing to the New Testament or the person of Jesus, who brought joy with him wherever he went. 'I have come that you may have life, life in all its fullness,' said Jesus. Those who entrust their lives to him know the truth of that claim. Francis Thompson's classic poem *The Hound of Heaven* describes his efforts to keep God out of his life because he thought God would spoil, not satisfy. He eventually found out his mistake.

Do you want a really satisfying life? The big three – money, sex and power – will not do it. They will not satisfy the deepest cravings of your heart. But, if you allow the love of God to enter you and work through you to others, you will begin a difficult life but a profoundly satisfying one. You'll be doing what you were made for.

iv. Money

'born to shop'

materialism

Materialism is the governing philosophy of the twentieth century. We are preoccupied with money, whether we are poor or rich. We are captivated by the passion to possess more and more things. Who says you can't have it all – with an American Express card? The consumer mentality has caught on around the globe: look at what has happened in Russia since the collapse of communism – all the worst forms of Western materialism. If there is one article of faith that marks the late twentieth century it is the conviction of our inalienable right to have more ... and more. Shopping has become the country's favourite pastime. With apologies to Descartes, it could be said, 'I shop, therefore I am', or, if you like, 'Tesco, ergo sum'. The main goal of the contemporary scene is financial success and a measure of security. Money has become a way of defining who we are by what we possess. When there are no values, money counts. Indeed, it counts so much that it has become a form of worship. You can understand a great deal about modern society from the shopping malls, which are our cathedrals to consumerism and affluence. 'Shopping malls, megacentres and commercial blocks are the temples of the new age,' writes Mike Starkey in *Born to Shop*.

> Speedbank machines are the wayside shrines where we perform our ritual devotions to the god which motivates us. The icons which offered medieval people the ultimate choice in life have given way to the shelves offering the ultimate in consumer choices ... In an earlier age life's adversity was met by a robust faith, even if it was only in human nature. Today we have our own solution. When the going gets tough, the tough go shopping (p. 83).

the emptiness of materialism

When we stop to look at the matter critically, it is hard not to agree that materialism is a peculiarly dangerous ideology. It is *false*, for one thing. People matter more than things, and people get squeezed out when economics is king. A good example of that is the true-life TV series *Hollywood Kids*, showing the emotional deprivation and inner emptiness of the poor rich children of film stars who have subordinated family relationships to the quest for fame and money. They are not unique: a great many people in Britain today feel their parents offer them toys but not time, and they are impoverished.

There's another problem. Materialism is *addictive*. The more you have the more you want. The Romans had a motto about it: 'Money is like sea water. The more you drink, the thirstier you become.'

What is more, materialism undoubtedly *hardens our sympathies*. Once we have settled for making money and possessions our priority, other people become secondary. And we do not care. Just too bad. In our lifetime we have seen two poisonous fruits of materialism. We have known the iron, unacceptable face both of communism and of consumerism. Surely there must be a better way to live than either of those?

Then there is a fundamental aspect to human nature which a materialistic lifestyle reveals as nothing else does. It is the paradox of hedonism: the pursuit of pleasure is *self-defeating*. There is in the human heart an emptiness that nothing transient can fill. I am sure you have felt it in your own life: that emptiness which comes with Christmas afternoon! The richest people in the world feel it too. Paul Getty Sr, the wealthiest man in his generation, had five marriages. He did not marry a sixth time because an astrologer told him, 'You will only live a short time after a sixth marriage,' and he wanted to be a hundred. This, by the way, was when he was

aged 84. He lived in a house protected by dogs. He was terrified of solitude but equally terrified by people. He lived to work. The world's richest man was bankrupt inside. He is no exception. Sinead O'Connor was blunt about it. 'As a race we feel empty. That is because our spirituality has been wiped out ... As a result we fill that gap with alcohol, drugs, sex or money.'

No, materialism does not satisfy, and *it does not last*. To rely on wealth is most unwise. A collapse in the Stock Market can wipe it all away overnight. Unemployment stalks the land, and it can strike in the boardroom as sharply as it does on the shop floor. Illness can remove all pleasure in our vaunted possessions. And to travel in a Third World country makes us profoundly aware of the injustice in the distribution of wealth, and shames us for our greed. To reflect on what consumerism is doing to our planet is an important warning against the perils of materialism. The acquisitive appetite which we have let loose in our Western societies has turned around to destroy us.

In fact, materialism ruins not only our environment but ourselves. It is highly *destructive* of all that is best in our characters, and often leads to envy, lust, luxury, greed, murder and suicide, as the British film *Shallow Grave* illustrates. It undermines what is true and beautiful in us, and acts like a slow poison. As G. K. Chesterton put it so forcefully:

> A person who is dependent upon the luxuries of this life is a corrupt person, spiritually corrupt, politically corrupt, financially corrupt. Christ said that to be rich is to be in a peculiar danger of moral wreck.

a better way

Those words of Chesterton bring us face to face with Jesus and his standard for life. It was said of him by one of his early followers, 'Though he was rich, yet for our sake he became

poor, so that we through his poverty might become rich.' The writer goes on to speak of the riches of character, of generosity, of love that Christ brings about in his followers. Christ's whole life was a protest against materialism. A man's life, he maintained, does not consist in the multitude of his possessions. And he told a marvellous story to back it up. There was a rich entrepreneur whose farming had been particularly successful. He was planning massive expansion, with a view to settling down in due course to a luxurious retirement. 'But God said to him, "You fool, tonight you are going to die. And then all the things you have prepared – whose will they be?" ' A heart attack carries him off in the night and all the baubles he has spent his life amassing are left for someone else. Fool indeed!

Money has become the opiate of the people. The obsessive pursuit of wealth is a modern pathology. We need a far bigger and richer vision than personal consumerism. Economics is no proper indicator of who we are.

One of the most powerful statements on this subject in recent years has been made by Aleksandr Solzhenitsyn. The old man, who had learned his wisdom in a prison camp, was addressing the wealthy young students who had gained their laurels at Harvard. At the Graduation Address in 1978 this was his advice:

> If humanism were right in declaring that man is born to be happy, he would not be born to die. Since his body is doomed to die his task on earth ... must be of a more spiritual nature. It cannot be the unrestrained enjoyment of everyday life. It cannot be the search for the best ways to obtain material goods and then cheerfully to get the most out of them. It has to be the fulfilment of a permanent earnest duty so that one's life journey may become an experience of moral growth, so that one may leave life a better human being than when one started it.

Solzhenitsyn found the key to that transformation in Jesus Christ. He made a thoughtful, well-considered choice. Was he right?

v. standards

whatever happened to right and wrong?

relativism

We were sitting in a pub having lunch and discussing morals. 'It was so much easier when I was young,' said my friend. 'We knew what was right, even though we didn't always do it.' Not so today. We make up our morality as we go along. It's not just that we break the rules; it's that we each want to make the rules. There's no such thing as 'right', only what seems right to me. And that may be very different, of course, from what seems right to you.

Relativism holds enormous influence these days. Indeed, it is almost taken for granted. It makes few moral demands on us because we can reduce our standards to what we feel disposed to do. It allows us to ditch almost every virtue in the book, if we so wish, apart from tolerance: to breach that is the ultimate sin, because tolerance justifies my doing what I want and not being blamed for it. Not only is it very appealing, but it accords with the enormous variety of cultures which jostle together in our streets. You do your thing. I'll do mine. But don't bug me. What's wrong with that?

objections to relativism

A lot is wrong with it. First and foremost, it doesn't make sense. Wonderfully liberating, no doubt, to cry, 'There are no absolute standards. Everything is relative.' But nonsense just the same. Because the person who makes this claim clearly expects us to accept it as the *truth*! Everything must be thought of as relative except the claim that everything is

relative. That relativist argument claims absolute status. The claim is totally bogus.

But there are far more serious objections to relativism. To make your standards up at your own preference leads inexorably to the breakdown of society. We are seeing it in our country today when crime has risen to the highest level ever, especially among young offenders. Ron Bibby, the Canadian sociologist, describes the situation graphically in his book about Canadian society in two words: 'mosaic madness'. Individualism run riot. No cohesion. That is what happens if you have no objective norms.

And of course relativism leads to unalloyed selfishness, destructive of others and also of ourselves. The French have a term for it, *anomie*. It is the malaise which is widespread in society – a sense of lostness, an emotional sickness which comes from living without guidelines. It is alienation, which is so marked a characteristic of our day. 'Money, success, it's all meaningless. I'm dead inside. I feel a thousand years old. I am bored with so much, even with my money.' That was Lyle Stewart, a pornography baron, but it might well have been written by any other successful person. As Noel Coward put it in one of his plays, 'The past depresses me, the present bores me, and the future scares me to death.'

three culture-watchers

On the larger scale, the dangers of relativism are very obvious. If there are no objective moral standards restraining men and nations, they are free to do what they want. 'Is there no God? Then everything is permitted.' That is how Dostoevsky saw it in *The Brothers Karamazov*. He was right. That is how atheistic communism acted in Russia when they raped Czechoslovakia and Afghanistan. That was the philosophy of the Nazis when they decided to go for a pure Aryan race and liquidate six million Jews. And do you remember the attitude of the Nazi war criminals when

brought to trial? 'I was just following orders.'

A century ago the atheist Friedrich Nietzsche saw very clearly that if God and traditional values were eliminated the strong could impose their will on the rest. That led him to the model of the superman and the ethic of the 'will-to-power'. This century has been playing out that scenario, in Russia and Germany, Serbia and Vietnam. Ours has been the bloodiest century in all history. Maybe William Penn was right: 'Nations must be governed by God or they will be ruled by tyrants.' History has yet to produce a single example of relativism providing enlightened and benevolent government. And if it is not good for the state, it can't be good for the individual, however seductive it appears.

One of the most powerful and perceptive books of the twentieth century is William Golding's *Lord of the Flies*. In it he shows the disastrous, indeed murderous, results of human nature unrestrained by any objective morals – even when that nature belongs to a bunch of schoolchildren. Relativism in morals simply will not do. It is the recipe for chaos. And it is certainly not something that is self-evidently correct. Far from it. The nations of the world do not just go for any old values: they are remarkably agreed upon virtues which they accept as valid and try to promote: bravery, honesty, marital fidelity, care for children, politeness – all these are qualities recommended in practically every culture and religion. It is flying in the face of all the evidence to suppose that moral relativism is the route to progress. It is the way to extinction.

the ultimate refutation

In Jesus of Nazareth we have the supreme example of a life which displays all the virtues known to human beings, and none of the vices. That character has been the inspiration for most of the best art, music, medicine and character down the succeeding two millennia. Are we to trash it and say that, in the light of relativism and its current political correctness, it

is a matter of indifference whether we go for the standards of Jesus or those of Hitler and Stalin? Are we reduced to the moral swamps of relativism? Or is there some solid rock standing out of the morass? Could it be that the Absolute has come into the world of the relative? Could it be that the best of all advice would be to follow his invitation to life at its best, 'Come, follow me'?

real lives

Alice Pitt-Pitts *recently studied Modern History. Whilst a student, she spent much of her time on the river rowing for her college and the Oxford University blues boat.*

Despite the fact that I come from a Christian background, where both my parents are committed Christians, the full meaning of Christianity never got through to me. I thought it was about going to church, being good and saying your prayers at bedtime. When I started as a student, I began going to one of the town-centre churches out of force of habit. It was full of hundreds of students. One morning after the service the woman next to me turned round, her face shining with joy, and said, 'Isn't it wonderful that there are so many people here this morning to worship Jesus?' Her words made me aware of a huge gulf between us. She had something – a real living faith – that I did not have. I felt a fraud for being there and stopped going to church after that.

The following term, there was a Christian Union mission, and I went along to listen out of curiosity. For the first time

I realized that Christianity is all about a relationship with Jesus. Our sin separates us from him, but he took the punishment we deserve, dying in our place so that our relationship can be restored. Provided we ask for his forgiveness and are prepared to turn from our old ways and give him control of our lives, we can have a relationship with him and receive eternal life.

Later that evening I also read a booklet called *Why Jesus?*, which made it clear that none of my excuses for delaying in dealing with this were valid. I realized that sitting on the fence was impossible and unrealistic, and to do so would be a decision against Christ. That night I became a Christian.

It would be wrong to pretend the Christian life is easy. It is a bit like rowing against the tide (of the world's normal ways of living) rather than just floating down stream. The Christian life is not an easy way out. However, it is true to say that I have been healed and transformed by my relationship with Jesus. My outlook on life and what is important has completely changed. Becoming a Christian is the best thing that has ever happened to me.

vi. religion

one mountain, many paths?

One of the most pervasive ideologies of our day is pluralism. Let's be clear what we are talking about. All Western countries are 'plural' societies these days, with a variety of cultures, faiths and races. We must distinguish this plurality from *pluralism*. This is an ideology which makes a fundamental distinction between facts and values. Facts are public, while values and beliefs are private, and very diverse. In this realm there are no norms. You have your views and I have mine. They are all

equally valid – and equally relative. Certainty in matters of religion is impossible and would be undesirable anyhow, because it would prove socially disruptive. All religions lead to God. Sincerity, not truth, is the important thing (anyway, what is truth?). Tolerance is what matters.

Against this background all truth claims are suspect, and none more than the Christian insistence that Jesus is the Way to God, the Truth about God, and the very Life of God. To talk like that is narrow, intolerant and fanatical. It is clearly untenable. OK. Let's have a good look at pluralism.

the challenge of pluralism

It is often suggested that modern thought has rendered historic Christianity untenable – we are more sophisticated these days. But a moment's reflection will show that this is not the case. As soon as monotheism broke into the world with the ancient Jews, it had to face all the challenges of pluralism. The Canaanites and all the rest swarmed around the little country of Israel like bees, all with different beliefs, and sought to swamp Jewish faith in one holy God or else to assimilate it to their own myths. Judaism held out resolutely against both expedients.

It was just the same with the first Christians. They were Jews, every one of them, but they went further, and were utterly persuaded that this one true God had showed his hand – no, his whole being – in the person of Jesus of Nazareth. God had come to seek humankind and draw us back to himself. This was no myth or private value-judgment. It was sober history and sober truth. Indeed, it was the most important truth in the world. They were clear that there was *one* way of acceptance with God, depending not on religious pedigree or moral achievement but on his undreamed-of generosity. All this they maintained with a fearless courage in the face of a religious pluralism which makes our version look mild.

Naturally they were unpopular. But had they gone for one

of the politically correct religious attitudes under the Empire, they would not have been persecuted; nobody would have bothered them. The Romans had broad views on religion. When they conquered your territory they tended either, like the Hindus, to add your special deity to the existing pantheon, or else to identify him, as modern pluralists would, with a deity of their own who fulfilled the same function. This the Christians resolutely refused to do. They were convinced that they were on to the truth, and they refused to give it up. That is why all hell broke loose in vilification and spasmodic persecution. There's nothing new about pluralism.

the weakness of pluralism

Pluralism makes some very strange assumptions. It assumes that *Christians are arrogant* and want to push their views on everybody else. Not so. Christians believe that Jesus is alive today, and they want to share this news with everyone else, modestly but confidently. And that is very different from arrogance.

Another assumption is that *all religions lead to God*. That sounds wonderfully liberal, but it is sheer nonsense all the same. How can all religions lead to God when some of them do not believe in a personal God at all, like Buddhism, while others believe in many gods, like animism? Some believe in an inscrutable deity who cares nothing about the world he set in progress, some believe in a vengeful deity who is out to get us, while Christianity maintains God is personal, loving, and active for our rescue. The whole idea of 'God' is different in these conflicting viewpoints.

Another of the strange assumptions of pluralism is that *sincerity is all you need*. Believe anything sincerely, and you will be fine. What an utterly cynical creed! I may sincerely believe that a bottle of whisky a day is good for me, and act on it, but that will not prevent cirrhosis of the liver. Sincerity is no guarantee of truth. We can be sincere and wrong.

Want another false assumption? It is that *all religious experience is basically the same*. Who says? The Western liberal, of course. But a Muslim fundamentalist killing Christians in Northern Nigeria may not be having at all the same religious experience as the animist seeking to buy off evil spirits, or the Hindu guru meditating on reality. And if you ask converts from other faiths they will tell you in no uncertain terms that much as they value their hereditary background, the experience they have of God as Christians is radically different from anything they ever experienced before; particularly in the areas of knowing God personally, having an assurance of forgiveness, and an inner joy and peace they cannot but attribute to the Holy Spirit whom they have welcomed within them.

And you know, it is very arrogant of us Western people airily to dismiss all other religions as the same, or going in the same direction. Is the Satanist going in the same direction as Mother Teresa did? Ask the adherents of Islam in the Gulf if all religions lead to God and if it does not much matter which you follow. It is Western liberals who tell us that all religions go the same way, not the adherents of these faiths themselves – still less Jesus of Nazareth. His lifestyle was very humble, but his claims were majestic: he saw himself as bringing God on to the stage of human history, no less. And that is a wildly different claim from the founder of any other faith. It is either right or wrong.

the impotence of pluralism

I have another problem with this fashionable pluralism. It is morally defective. It has no help to offer us with our ethical struggles. Pluralism accepts the vast varieties of ethical standards and religious beliefs on offer. On its view, you pick and choose, whether it is euthanasia, genetic engineering or sexual practice. And anything goes: it is all OK. Pluralism gives you no guiding star, and no moral power.

the evasion of pluralism

Worst of all, pluralism is totally allergic to the issue of truth. The true believer is the real danger, because he or she claims to be right. But what if he or she *is* right? Galileo claimed to be right, and was given a terrible time for it by the religious establishment of the day. But he *was* right, and everyone now recognizes as much. What if the Christians are right? What if there is a living God who made the world and all that is in it? What if he does love us so much that he came to reveal himself to us in a human life? What if he did burden himself with our moral filth at the cross? What if he does offer the power of his resurrection life to those (of whatever faith and none) who will accept it? There is a massive truth question here, and it will not go away.

What are you going to make of it?

real lives

When **Simon Jordan** *studied Geography at university, he also helped out at his local BBC radio station. Since graduating, he has (among other things) had a job as a traffic and travel news presenter on local radio.*

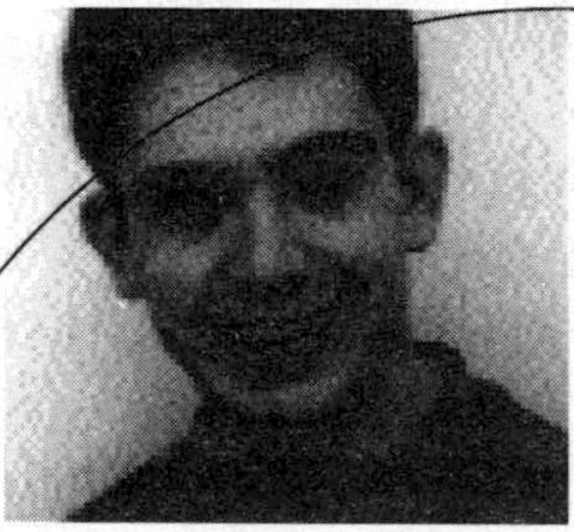

Religion has nothing whatsoever to do with Christianity. Sounds crazy? Well, when I arrived as a fresher I would have said exactly the opposite. As far as I was concerned, going to church and being a Christian were the same thing – you did both on Sunday, and kept quiet about the fact for the rest of the week.

But what I soon discovered on beginning at university is that religious habit and real Christianity couldn't be more different. I may have known the routine of church, but I didn't know Jesus Christ for myself.

What really impressed me was meeting Christians my own age who were clear on what they believed and why they believed it, and who also had the integrity to live that out. This put to shame what was beginning to look like rather empty religious performance on my part. The words came easily – much harder was meaning them. More worrying, I knew there was a yawning gap between the moral principles I was prepared to sign up to and my track record at putting them into practice.

In fact, all my religion succeeded in doing was deceiving people and deluding myself – and the cracks were beginning to show. At least I realize that now.

It was only because these new Christian friends of mine took time to talk with me – and because I was ready to listen – that I heard and understood the truth about Jesus. It was amazing news. Forgiveness, purpose in life now, and certainty beyond death had all been made possible through Jesus' death on the cross and his resurrection. As they explained, what my religious effort could never achieve, Jesus Christ alone could bring, if I trusted him.

In the end I realized I had a choice. But when it came to the decision between living the truth and living the lie, I realized that there was really only one honest option open. I decided to ask God for forgiveness. Towards the end of my first year, I stopped going my own way and turned around to Jesus. I simply asked him to include me in his rescue and gave my life up to live for him.

4 the 'J' file

'the truth is out there'

Fellini, the celebrated Italian film director, typically posed this view of life with tongue in cheek: 'Like many people,' he wrote, 'I have no religion. I am just sitting on a small boat, drifting with the tide. I just go on cutting, editing, shooting, looking at life, trying to make others see that today we stand naked and more defenceless than at any time in history. What I am waiting for I do not know – perhaps the Martians will come to save us.' He was not alone in this thought.

Just think of the way the *Star Wars* films, *Close Encounters* and *ET* itself engaged the popular imagination. Think of the continuing grip of *Star Trek* on its 'trekkies'. Even as I write, the science-fiction programme which gains the highest ratings on BBC2 is *The X Files*, a drama investigating UFOs and the paranormal, while SF authors crowd the bookshelves. Harmless imagination, to be sure. But it is also highly significant. Many thoughtful people like Fellini despair of the mess we have got the world into and are longing for an answer, for truth, for a

rescuer from outside of us. An extraterrestrial. But we know in our heart of hearts that it is a vain hope.

Curiously enough, the Christian faith is all about an extraterrestrial. Jesus Christ claims to be just that: a rescuer from outside of us who can make a real difference to our lives, our society and our world if we allow him to do so. The truth is out there, but we can't get to it. It has to come to us. The Christian claim is that the truth has indeed come in Jesus of Nazareth. But will that claim stand critical examination? Or will Jesus prove, on careful assessment, to be just as insubstantial as Fellini's Martians?

Fortunately, we are provided with a considerable amount of evidence to enable us to answer that question. Let's examine it under three headings. Can we trust the New Testament text? Can we trust the sources? Can we trust the story?

I. can we trust the text of the New Testament?

I keep bumping into a myth, as I chat with students. Someone has told them that the New Testament manuscripts are late and therefore unreliable, and have been heavily tampered with over the years. This myth has a very interesting origin. In 1842 a German theologian, Bruno Bauer, was deprived of his chair on account of his wildly unorthodox opinions. It was Bauer's view that Jesus never lived, but was a figment of the imagination of the evangelist Mark, written up at the end of the second century AD.

The truth is very different. We are better placed to assess the reliability of the manuscript tradition in the case of the New Testament than any other ancient book. No ancient document has come down to us with such a wealth of manuscripts to back it up as the Gospels. We have copies of the Gospels going back to well within a century of their composition in the latter part of the first century AD. This may sound like a long time, but it is fantastic compared with classical

authors of the period! The gap, for example, between when Tacitus wrote (about fifty years after the evangelists) and the earliest surviving manuscript of his work is some 800 years. With the historian Livy, a near contemporary of the evangelists, the gap is 1,100 years. In striking contrast with the two or three manuscripts we have attesting the text of these secular writers, we have literally hundreds of manuscripts of the New Testament. They are written in many languages, and they come from all over the ancient world. They give us the text of the New Testament with astonishing agreement between them (just as the Isaiah scrolls found at Qumran precisely confirm the text of our previous earliest manuscript of Isaiah, though they antedate it by more than a thousand years). Of course, there are many variant readings in this vast array of manuscripts, all copied out laboriously by hand. But those who have studied the subject would all agree on these two central points.

First, no single doctrine of the New Testament depends on a disputed reading. And second, the text of the New Testament is so certain that no competent scholar would dream of making a conjectural emendation (*i.e.* a guess about what the text *should* read), common though that is in the case of classical texts. The strength of the manuscript tradition makes such a procedure impossible.

We actually possess (in Manchester, of all places!) a fragment of the Gospel of John which experts date between AD 100 and 125. And it is now very probable that we have a fragment of Mark's Gospel, hidden in one of the caves at Qumran, which dates back to before AD 68 when the community was overrun by the Romans, and the cave sealed up. We have all four Gospels in papyrus books well before AD 200. A document called *The Unknown Gospel* was discovered some years ago, written before AD 150: it draws heavily on our four Gospels, and so shows the authoritative position they had already attained by that time. The early heretic Valentinus, whose *Gospel of Truth*, written about AD 130, also turned up a

few decades ago, quoted the New Testament writings extensively. So did the Church Fathers Polycarp and Clement of Rome, thirty or forty years earlier.

By the end of the first century, that is to say within the lifetime of some who had known Jesus, the New Testament books were not only written, but were on their way to being collected together. And from the outset the New Testament was seen as authoritative information about Jesus. So authoritative that the Christians quoted it with the same reverence that they gave to the Old Testament. So authoritative that the heretics knew they must quote it extensively if they were going to get a hearing for their heresies.

This all enabled Professor Kenyon, the celebrated biblical archaeologist, to conclude: 'The interval between the dates of the original composition and the earliest extant evidence becomes so small as to be negligible, and the last foundation for any doubt that the Scriptures have come down to us substantially as they were written has now been removed' (*The Bible and Archaeology*, p. 288).

2. can we trust the sources?

Although most of what we know about Jesus is contained in Christian writings, there is corroboration from non-Christian sources, and it will be convenient to begin with these. They are certainly not prejudiced in favour of the Christian cause!

the non-Christian sources

First there is the evidence from early Roman writers. There is not a lot of it. You would not expect wealthy men of letters in Rome to take a great deal of notice of a carpenter who lived for a few years in Judea, on the edge of the map. What there is, however, is remarkable.

Tacitus, the great historian of the early Empire, wrote his *Annals* at the very beginning of the second century. In them

he gives a careful year-by-year account of affairs in Rome. When he gets to the year AD 64, when much of Rome was burnt down, he makes it plain that he agrees with the generally held view that Nero was responsible, because he wanted to redevelop a large area in the centre of the city as his palace.

> To dispel this rumour, Nero substituted as culprits and treated with the most extreme punishment some people, popularly known as Christians, whose disgraceful activities were notorious. The originator of the name, Christ, had been executed when Tiberius was emperor by order of the procurator Pontius Pilate. But the deadly cult, though checked for a time, was now breaking out again not only in Judea, the birthplace of this evil, but even throughout Rome, where all nasty and disgusting ideas from all over the world pour in and find a ready following.
> *(Annals 15.44).*

Obviously Tacitus does not know a lot about Christians. He does not like them, but he is clear they did not burn down Rome. He has a basic knowledge of 'the originator of the name' who was born in Judea, lived under the principate of Tiberius (AD 14–37) and was executed by Pilate (who governed the province AD 26–36). Tacitus knows there were lots of Christians in Rome as early as the sixties.

More comes from Pliny the Younger, a contemporary of Tacitus, who was sent in AD 112 to govern Bithynia in Northern Turkey. He kept referring everything to the emperor Trajan, and the correspondence survives. He writes one long letter about Christians (*Letters* 10.96). They were spreading like wildfire in his province. Christianity was becoming a social and economic problem. The pagan temples were closing down for lack of customers, the sacred festivals were becoming deserted, and the demand for sacrificial animals had

ceased. So Pliny executed those who refused to renounce their Christian allegiance. But he had qualms about it. That is why he wrote to Trajan. He had discovered that nothing improper went on in the Christian assemblies. Their whole guilt lay in refusing to worship the imperial statue and images of the gods, and in their habit of meeting on a fixed day, Sunday, to sing hymns to Christ as God. Their lives, he wrote, were exemplary. You would not find fraud, adultery, theft or dishonesty among them. To be sure, Pliny tells us nothing specific about Jesus himself. But he is clear that the 'Jesus movement' is a major force in this upland province adjoining the Black Sea. This secular governor gives testimony to the quality of life among the Christians, their weekly worship of Christ as God, their unwillingness to accord that status to others (even the emperor), their innocence and their phenomenal spread.

Writers of the stature of Pliny and Tacitus make the historicity of Jesus certain, and confirm some of the evidence we find laid out at much greater length in the Gospels.

We also find references to Jesus in Jewish literature of the time. The most remarkable comes from a Jewish guerrilla commander, Flavius Josephus, who fought the invading Romans in the war of AD 66–70, and subsequently turned historian and tried to restore the reputation of his countrymen in Roman eyes. He tells us a little about characters we find in the Gospels: Herod, Caiaphas, John the Baptist, James 'the brother of the so-called Christ'. But most significant of all is his extended reference to Jesus himself. It is worth quoting in full.

And there arose about this time [he means Pilate's time as governor, AD 26–36] Jesus, a wise man if indeed one should call him a man. For he was the performer of astonishing deeds, a teacher of those who are happy to receive the truth. He won over many Jews and also many Greeks. He was the Christ. And when Pilate had condemned

him to the cross at the instigation of our own leaders, those who had loved him at first did not give up. For he appeared to them on the third day alive again, as the holy prophets foretold, and had said many other wonderful things about him. And still to this day the race of Christians, so called after him, has not died out.

(*Antiquities 18.3.3*)

Needless to say, such powerful attestation from so hostile a source as Josephus is amazing, and has attracted enormous suspicion from those who cannot believe it to be genuine. But this testimony, in full, is to be found in all the surviving manuscripts of Josephus, and Eusebius read it there in the fourth century AD. No doubt some of it is sarcastic: 'If indeed one should call him a man' might be a snide allusion to his divine claims. 'He was the Christ' might allude to the charge affixed to his cross, 'Jesus of Nazareth, Jewish Messiah'. But it remains a solid, textually reliable reference to the founder of Christianity by Josephus (himself a late contemporary of Jesus). It alludes to his messiahship, his wisdom, his teaching, his miracles, his many conversations, his death and resurrection – not to mention the continuation of the movement.

Jewish, Roman and archaeological sources provide a good many more scraps of information about Jesus, but this is not the moment to go into them, except perhaps to summarize what they tell us. We learn that Jesus was born of a virgin, performed miracles, and was executed by Pilate on the cross, in thick darkness, at passover time. We learn that he had claimed to be God, and that he would depart and come again. He was the Christ. He rose from the tomb. He had disciples, who worshipped him as God.

His movement spread rapidly throughout the Roman world within a generation. His essential message could be distilled in this cryptogram, *ichthus*, meaning 'fish'. It stood for *Jesus Christ, Son of God, Saviour.*

the Christian sources

Very well, you may say, but what about the Christian evidence in the Gospels? Can we trust it? There are good reasons to suppose that we can.

First, no books in all the world's literature have been scrutinized so sharply over two and a half centuries as the Gospels. Today their credibility stands as high as ever. They emerge from every test with the utmost credit. That is an excellent reason for taking with the utmost seriousness the portrait they offer us of Jesus.

Second, there is a remarkable harmony in the general picture they present – as different from second-century imitations as chalk is from cheese.

Third, what we read in the Gospels fits closely with the secular evidence we have sketched above. But of course it fills it out and puts flesh on it. What is more, it chimes in precisely with what Paul, the great apostle, tells us in his references to the historical Jesus. Paul wrote in the fifties and the early sixties, before the earliest of the Gospels. His allusions are all the more impressive because they are so casual. He is not trying to prove anything, or teach his readers new things about Jesus. He is simply reminding them of what they had heard when they first became Christians some years earlier. It would hardly be possible to have better or earlier supporting evidence for the trustworthiness of the Gospels.

Fourth, the survival of eyewitnesses of Jesus' ministry is an important factor to bear in mind when we are assessing the reliability of the Gospels. If the Gospel-writers had been telling exaggerated stories about what Jesus did and said, there were still plenty of people around at the time of their publication who could have pointed out the errors. And in that case the Gospels would not have gained the universal circulation and recognition that they did. The eyewitnesses could not fault the records: they were reliable.

There are other ways of checking the trustworthiness of

these remarkable little books. If the church had cooked up the contents of the Gospels, we should have expected them to put into Jesus' mouth statements about matters of burning concern to themselves. On the contrary we find that these problem issues for the early church (such as the lordship of Jesus, overtly supernatural occurrences in church life, the controversy over the place of circumcision, and whether Christians should eat food that had been offered to idols) are conspicuous by their absence. That gives me a lot of confidence that the Gospel-writers were giving a true record and not making up things which would have suited them.

The parables provide another very interesting insight into the reliability of the Gospel-writers. People sometimes wonder if these parables go back to Jesus himself or whether the early Christians made them up. But why should anyone have pretended that Jesus taught in this remarkable way if he did not? Who could have been the genius to create them if not he? One thing is very clear. Although some rabbinic examples exist, nobody before him had taught in parables like Jesus. And nobody after him was able to do so, either. The early church did not preach in parables; but they knew, and faithfully recorded, that Jesus had done so.

There are two critical tools of which the New Testament scholars are rightly fond. One they call the 'criterion of multiple attestation'. It simply means that there is added reason to accept the authenticity of some event or saying if it is recorded in more than one strand of the Gospel tradition. Very well, apply that to the astounding story of Jesus feeding five thousand people from a few rolls and sardines. It is in all four Gospels. You could not have more impeccable evidence for even something so amazing as that. It is not the evidence about Jesus that is at issue: but whether we will go where the evidence points us.

The other tool is the matter of Aramaic. This was the language of Palestine in Jesus' day: Jesus habitually used it. The Aramaic experts have discovered a remarkable thing. Much of

the teaching of Jesus can easily be translated back from the Greek into the underlying Aramaic, and then it falls into rhyming cadences. This is very rare and very beautiful. It is also very memorable. That may account for the close verbal similarity, even identity, which we find in some of Jesus' teaching as recorded in different Gospels. Jews learnt by memorizing, and this rhyming Aramaic which underlies parts of our Gospels (and occasionally peeps out in words like *talitha cumi* and *abba*) is highly memorable. No doubt Jesus taught in this way because he wanted his teaching to be carefully remembered and accurately passed on. We have every reason to believe that it was.

3. can we trust the story?

But granted that the story of Jesus was reliably transmitted, can we believe it? That is the problem. Sublime the story certainly is, but is it credible? I suppose the heart of our problem resolves itself into two main questions. Was Jesus more than man? And did he rise from the grave? Let us take those two in turn.

was Jesus more than man?

The Jews, the original people among whom Jesus walked and talked, were passionate monotheists, the hardest people in all the world to convince that he was more than man. Yet vast numbers of them became convinced. I think these seven elements proved decisive for them – as they could be for us.

First, his character. It has dominated humankind from that day to this, appealing equally to men and women, young and old, all types and nationalities. To zoologists, lawyers and engineers. To public-school and state-school types. To northerners and southerners alike. He had all the virtues known to humankind and none of the vices. There was something magnetically attractive about that life of his, as you will sense if

you read through a Gospel with an open mind. For instance, he treated women and children with a welcome and respect unparalleled in antiquity. Men left their work to flock around him. What was there in his heredity and environment that could explain such a character?

Second, his teaching. It is the most wonderful the world has ever known. Nothing like it has emerged before or since. Its profundity, its pungency, its clarity, its authority set it apart from all other teaching. How do you explain that in a wandering carpenter?

Third, his lifestyle. He taught the highest standards of conduct and, unlike any other human being before or since, he kept them. He never needed to apologize – to man or to God. That is utterly unique. He claimed to be without sin, that inner failure which stains all the rest of us. Every strand of the New Testament shows that his followers, who knew him intimately, agreed. And remember the French proverb, 'No man is a hero to his valet.' This man was! Even his enemies, Judas, Pilate, Caiaphas and the Pharisees, could throw no mud at him that stuck.

Fourth, his miracles. These are not an embarrassment to Christians. They are added indications of who Jesus was. These miracles are embedded in almost all strands of the evidence about Jesus, reaching back as it does to within a few years of his life: there is Jewish attestation as well. It is fascinating to contrast people's credulity about ETs and UFOs with their scepticism about the miracles of Jesus which are so firmly documented. The miracles were done for the benefit of others, never for selfish ends. They are no mere mighty deeds: they illustrate and underline his claims. For instance, when he feeds the multitude he wants people to realize that he is the real nourishment for our lives. When he heals a blind man, he wants to show them that he can open eyes that are spiritually blind. Similarly, when he raises a man from death it is to underline his claim to be 'the resurrection and the life'. Those miracles of his do not by themselves prove his deity,

but they are highly congruous with it.

Fifth, his fulfilment of prophecy. Literally scores of Old Testament prophecies and predictions found their fulfilment in Jesus of Nazareth. There is no parallel to that anywhere in the history of the world. Different Old Testament concepts like Son of Man, Son of God, the anointed prophet, priest and king, and many more, intersect in him and in him alone. He is even portrayed as the replacer of the Jewish law. Many of the prophecies concerned his birth and his death – and those are the two hardest areas in which to fake fulfilment. His birth from a virgin, at Bethlehem: his death, despised and rejected, among criminals, undertaken to deal with human sins, followed by burial in a rich man's tomb, crowned by resurrection and ascent to the throne of God – who could arrange their schedule to fulfil all that?

Sixth, his claims. They are outrageous, indeed mad, if they are not true. Despite his personal humility and simplicity of life, he made claims which no other man has ever dared to make. He claimed that God was his '*Abba*' (an utterly unique filial relationship, like 'daddy'), and that whoever had seen him had seen the Father. He claimed the right to forgive human sins, to be worshipped, to be the final judge of humankind, to be the way to God, the truth about God and the very life of God embodied in human flesh. What are we to make of claims like these?

Finally, his death. It is the most famous death in the world. Millions carry the reminder of it in a cross around their neck. Jesus did not, like some modern religious fundamentalists, court martyrdom. He sweated blood at the prospect of death. Yet the unselfishness of that death, its self-sacrifice, its sin-bearing, its triumph, drew all sorts of people to him, and still does. The fact that so perfect a person went willingly to such a terrible death, coupled with the interpretation which he gave it (to liquidate the sins of the whole world) convinced them. It lent enormous force to Jesus' own question: 'Who do you say that I am?'

did Jesus rise from the dead?

But what about the resurrection? The Christian claim hangs, to a large extent, upon its truth or falsehood. How are we to approach what is on the face of it a preposterous claim? We must come at it with an open mind. That is vital. The Christian tends to say, 'It is in the Bible. That's good enough for me.' The sceptic is inclined to say, 'Dead men don't come back.' Both Christian and doubter must lay aside prejudice, and look at the evidence. It seems to me that five facts cohere, and all point in the same direction.

First, Jesus was dead. The point would not be worth making were it not for wild assertions which are sometimes made that he was not really dead, but revived in the cool of the tomb, and persuaded his followers of his resurrection. This is frankly incredible. You did not survive a Roman crucifixion: they were experts at this macabre form of execution. And in John's Gospel we are given a fascinating bit of eyewitness testimony: it says 'one of the soldiers pierced Jesus' side with a spear, bringing a sudden flow of blood and water' (John 19:34). The writer could not possibly have known the medical importance of his statement. But the separation of dark clot from clear serum is one of the strongest proofs of death. There can be no doubt that Jesus was dead.

Second, the tomb was empty. This is agreed all round. By Easter morning the body of Jesus was absent from the tomb in which he had been laid to rest on Friday. Who could have wanted to remove the body, and so give substance to the resurrection story? The only possible people would be his enemies or his friends. I ask you, would his enemies, who had spent three embarrassing years trying to get him put away, remove his body from the grave once they had, at last, got him where they wanted? Of course not. Then what about his friends? I don't see how they could. There was a guard of soldiers on the tomb and a massive rock over the entrance –

sealed for good measure. Read about it in Matthew 27:62–66. What is more, his followers would never have done such a thing, even if they could. It is psychologically impossible. Like all Jews, they believed that there would be a resurrection of everyone at the Day of Judgment, but not before. Dispirited at the execution of the one in whom they had pinned their hopes, they scattered to their homes after his death. They were certainly not expecting his resurrection. It is sometimes suggested that they were guilty of deliberate fraud, stealing the body and then pretending Jesus was alive again. That is beyond belief. They went around the Roman world for the rest of their lives boldly proclaiming the resurrection, despite appalling obstacles. They allowed themselves to be persecuted, imprisoned and killed for maintaining its truth. You don't go through all that for a fraud!

Third, the Christian church was born. It can be traced back to that first Easter. Something got it off the ground with enormous power and joy and confidence a few days after the execution of its founder. If not the resurrection, would you like to hazard a credible alternative? Initially there was nothing to distinguish them from the rest of Judaism apart from their burning conviction that Jesus was the long-awaited Messiah and had conquered death. This was the faith that set the entire Roman world ablaze.

Fourth, Jesus appeared extensively to his followers after his death. We have many accounts of the resurrection appearances of Jesus. Over a period of forty days he appeared to a wide variety of people in a wide variety of settings: the twelve disciples, James his unbelieving brother, Thomas the sceptic, Mary Magdalene his friend, Mary his mother, and no less than five hundred people at one time. Finally, he appeared to Saul of Tarsus, his determined enemy, and revolutionized his life. Read the accounts in Matthew 28, Mark 16, Luke 24, John 20 and 21, and 1 Corinthians 15:1–11, which is the earliest of them all. Read, and make up your own mind. Could these be hallucinations? Hallucinations do not happen to different

groups, in different places at different times. Moreover, they tend to be a mark of disintegration in the personality. But the resurrection appearances marked a new wholeness, a new confidence and joy, a new outreach in the disciples who had witnessed them. Read the Acts of the Apostles and see the sequel for yourself.

Finally, the crunch point. *Lives were transformed* by meeting this risen Jesus, and they still are. Think of Peter, changed from a coward and a turncoat at the crucifixion when he deserted Jesus, to a man of rock on whose courage and witness the early church was founded. Think of Saul of Tarsus, who met with the risen Jesus on the road to Damascus when he was on a mission to destroy Christians. He became the most passionate and intelligent Christian advocate the world has ever seen. Think of the disciples as a group. They had deserted Jesus in his hour of need, but after the first Easter they were prepared to take on the known world as they contended for the resurrection which had turned them from a rabble into a church.

When you consider honestly and soberly the change in the lives of these people, and of millions since all over the world from every background and nationality and culture; when you consider that they all put their transformation down to the resurrection; when you reflect on the remarkable fact that they did not simply claim that he rose from death but is alive today and they know him and communicate with him – then I think you will agree that we have very strong evidence that the resurrection story is true, and that Christ is a mighty force to be reckoned with today.

Is it hardly surprising that more than a third of the world's population professes allegiance to Jesus Christ?

real lives

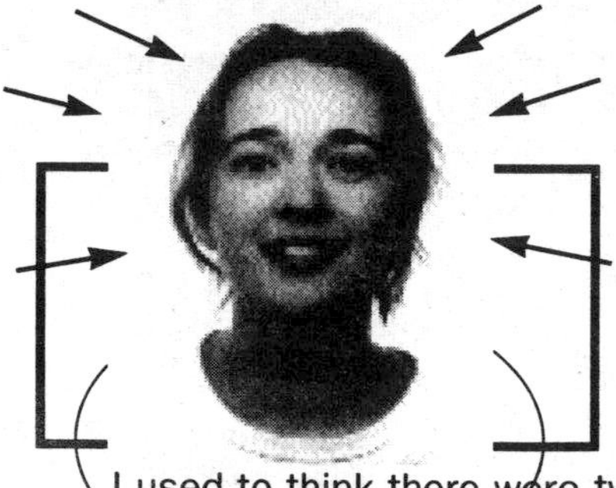

Mary Ambler *graduated in Classics. She now works as an executive for an 'ab fab' fashion PR firm in West London. She enjoys yacht racing and all things 70's.*

I used to think there were two types of Christians: one with a small 'c' and one with a big 'C'. I believed it was enough to live according to the Christian values of mere social convention. I was in the small 'c' category. Being a Christian with a big 'C' was, in my opinion, unnecessary – a lot of praying and singing in church for no apparent reason.

When I began as a student, I quickly got stuck in with a rowdy crowd of friends. We were dedicated party types. I was also busy running the University Sailing Club. In order to live life to the full I developed fairly decadent social habits – in short, I was an unashamed hedonist and I loved it!

In my 4th year most of my good friends had gone down and the pressure of Finals loomed. As I immersed myself in revision, my intellectual struggle in Philosophy was taking over every thought. It was at this stage that I began to have real doubts about my life; about what gave it meaning, about many of my friendships which turned out to be superficial. Inside I felt frustrated, let down and afraid.

I was challenged by Christianity at this time, much to my alarm. As I got to know a Christian friend, I found out I wasn't even a Christian with a small 'c', because Jesus Christ was not at the centre of my life. I also found that

Christianity held the answers to the baffling philosophical issues spinning around in my head.

Over the ensuring months of investigation I found that the historical evidence for Jesus' life, death and resurrection was convincing. But accepting these rational truths was insufficient. I wanted to respond to the earth-shattering fact that Christ had died for my sins on the cross. Handing the helm over to him was utter relief.

Jesus Christ is at the centre now, and my priority is to get to know him better, and to live for him as he gave his life for me. This has transformed my perspective on life, and my friendships. It also makes a real difference to how I deal with a pressurizing job and to my ultimate ambitions at work. None of this is easy, but I know God's plans for my future are good and I can trust him.

5 important questions

I. what is the heart of Christianity?

Curiously enough, there is a lot of confusion about the heart of Christianity.

Many people assume that if you are born in a Christian country you must be a Christian. But a moment's reflection will show that there is no such thing as a Christian country. All countries are an amalgam of diverse viewpoints, beliefs and behaviour patterns.

'Very well then, my parents are Christians. So I probably am, too.' Hang on: remember the many ways in which you are keen to be different from your parents! Maybe this is one of them? The commitment of my parents to, say, the Labour Party does not commit me, does it?

'I have been baptized as a baby: that makes me a Christian, does it not?' To be sure, baptism is the mark of belonging to Christ. The only problem is that we can have the sign without the reality. Millions do. We can sport the label on the bottle, so to speak, while the contents are very different. There's nothing wrong with the sign: we just haven't fulfilled the conditions of repentance and faith in Jesus which it signifies.

'I go to church from time to time: that must do it?' I think not. Remember how the greatest opponents of Jesus were the religious church people of his day. You can go daily into my house without becoming a member of my family, can you not? Well, we can do the same with God.

'But I live a Christian life – better than many who make a song and dance about it.' That is admirable: God naturally wants us to live good lives. But all sorts of people who make no claim to Christianity can be found living estimable lives. Being a Christian must be more than that.

The truth is that neither citizenship, creeds, ceremonies, churchgoing nor conduct can make a person a Christian – although a Christian will have a set of beliefs, be baptized, want to worship, and live a godly life.

The heart of being a Christian is obvious enough if you come to think about it. It is Christianity we are talking about. It is all about being a follower and even a friend of Jesus Christ – that is what he offers us (John 15:15). Christianity is not a religion at all, but rather a relationship with the most wonderful person who has ever lived – and, as any real Christian will tell you, he is still alive! This is what makes the relationship so fulfilling.

2. I do my best – what more could God ask?

This has been a common attitude all down the ages. Forgiveness, we instinctively feel, is never cheap, and so we must do something to earn it. It may be through mechanical ways like the Tibetan prayer wheel, animistic ways like ancestor worship, Buddhist ways like the Eightfold Path, or Western ways like trying harder and never doing anyone any harm. But, popular though it is, this road is a dead end. It is utterly misguided. Let me show you why.

In the first place, it is so shallow. It allows us to rely on

deeds not relationship. Would it satisfy any loving parents if their offspring kept the bedroom tidy (some hope!), and mowed the lawn but never gave them a hug? Of course not.

Listen to Jesus' analysis of human nature. There is nothing shallow about it. He penetrates to the heart of the human disease, our pride and self-centredness. He declares that 'from within, out of men's hearts, come evil thoughts, sexual immorality, theft, murder, adultery, greed, malice, deceit, lewdness, envy, slander, arrogance and folly. All these evils come from inside and make a man "unclean"' (Mark 7:21). Of course we know how to do good things. But that does not change the fundamental twist in our natures: 'you then, though you are evil, know how to give good gifts to your children ...' observed the great physician, Jesus Christ (Luke 11:13). You cannot get rid of cancer by using lots of make-up and running around helping everyone else in the house. Doing good deeds is a very shallow remedy for a very serious situation.

Secondly, it is impossible. You and I can't win God's favour by our own good deeds for the simple reason that they are not good enough. He is perfect. He is the moral ruler of the universe. And as for you and me – well, we screw up every day.

'What?' you say. 'I'm a good living person. I keep the Ten Commandments.' Really?

Let me ask you a few questions then. Have you kept the very first commandment, to give God the number one place in your life? Of course not. Or the second, not to make him in your own image? Don't we all do that, saying, 'The God I believe in is like this ...' rather than stopping to find out how he has revealed himself in the Bible? Try number three: you must not take the name of God in vain. Unfortunately we do it all the time. Or the fourth, keeping the sabbath holy: one day in seven kept special for God, the family and leisure? Don't make me laugh! Honour father and mother? Not likely! When we're young we rebel as hard as we can. When we're married, we neglect them. When they are old, we stuff them

into an old people's home. Honour them indeed!

I feel a bit better with the command not to kill – until I recall Jesus tracing the evil deed of murder to the evil source in the human heart and its hatreds (Matthew 6:21–22). No ground for smugness there.

It's the same with the adultery business. I may not have technically committed adultery, common though it is, but I have indulged in a variety of sexual behaviour that I would not like to defend before a holy God (Matthew 6:27–28). And so one could go on through the remaining commandments. I haven't been able to keep one of them perfectly. Have you?

Even if we could live an immaculate life from now until the day we die, what about the accusing past? When the Bible tells us that there is none righteous, no, not one, we can't quarrel with that. It simply is not possible for us to get through to God by doing good things. My best is not good enough for him.

Third, it is intolerable. If heaven were reserved for self-made men and women parading their fancied virtues under everyone else's nose, it would be hell. Ascot is bad enough, with everyone showing off their clothes for all they are worth. Is heaven to be one long Ascot? Perish the thought. Is man to say to God, 'Move over, God. Here I come'? Such an attitude would be unthinkable. It would leave us untouched in our pride and self-esteem. My good deeds can never make up for my crooked heart and my rebellious attitude towards the God I have wronged and have earnestly desired to evade. He has no room for big-heads in his family. There is one condition, for entry: one only. It is to change our attitude, come down off our high horse, and humbly beg his pardon.

3. why do Christians emphasize the cross?

Almost everyone assumes that God loves us and will be

merciful to us. But why? When I think of the trouble I have given him, and the lengths to which I have gone to argue that he does not even exist, I shall need something more than guesswork to assume that he is so well disposed towards me. Ask any animist in Africa or Asia. They are under no illusions that the other world is benevolent towards them. Why should God bother about the likes of us? What ground is there for supposing that he does?

Christians have been in no doubt about the answer. It is because of the death of Jesus Christ on a cross – the most horrifying way of death ever invented. The Romans reserved it for slaves and enemies: no citizen could be put to death that way. But thousands of people were killed by that ghastly torture. What is so special about the death of Jesus? And what significance is there in his death on a *cross*?

Let's take the first question first. The significance of the cross is the person who died on it. This was no criminal paying the just (if merciless) penalty for his crimes. This was God's own Son, the one who brought the unseen God into focus for us. The one who embodied as much of the divine nature as it was possible to embody in a human form. 'In Christ', wrote the apostle Paul with deep conviction, 'all the fulness of the Deity lives in bodily form' (Colossians 2:9). And if that is so, it shows us at once the importance of the cross. It means that God Almighty thinks us so valuable that he has not only come to this earth for us but has tasted our ultimate doom – death, as a young man in indescribable agony. Could God possibly have given a more compelling answer to the problem of suffering? *This* was the supremely innocent sufferer hanging on that cross. God may not have explained the problem of pain, but he came to share it. He is the suffering God. I can honour and worship a God like that.

But even this does not take us to the heart of the cross. So let us turn to the second of our two questions. Why should Jesus have died on a cross, rather than being beheaded or stoned to death? The answer is very interesting.

The Old Testament had made it very clear that anyone who died exposed on a stake was seen as resting under the judgment of God (Deuteronomy 21:22–23). Jesus had told his followers that he was going to give his life to ransom people like us who had been taken captive by evil in all its varied forms (Mark 10:45). Well, his death on a cross ('stake' was the word for it in the Greek, an unmistakable reference to the Deuteronomy text) showed that he willingly took on himself the fate of the guilty criminal, so that we who were guilty before God could know that we were accepted. He laid down his spotless life in the place of us – guilty rebels against the Father's love. The task was completed: Jesus had done all that was necessary to reconcile us to the God we had offended. So we can be not only forgiven but also, as the New Testament loves to call it, justified and acquitted (Romans 5:1). The past – with its accusing finger – has been dealt with. He, the innocent one, took the place of us, the guilty party. He bore the judgment that was ours by right, so that we might enjoy Christ's own status as children in the family of God. What an incredible exchange! Nowhere else in all the world's religions will you find a picture of God like this. To show his love, and to bring his rebellious subjects back to him, he endures the fate that they deserved, and the whole task has been completed, once and for all. It remains for us to come to God and thank him for what he has done. Listen to Peter: 'Christ died for sins once for all, the righteous for the unrighteous, to bring you to God' (1 Peter 3:18).

Once you see that, it takes your breath away. Did he love me that much?

Yes, Calvary proves it. 'The Son of God ... loved me and gave his life for me', sang the ex-persecutor Saul of Tarsus, once he had allowed that sacrificial love of Christ to make a new man of him (Galatians 2:20). That sets us free from the skeletons in our cupboard. It puts a new spring in our step and joy in our hearts. We can stand high. We matter to God Almighty. And we can be sure of forgiveness and acceptance

because it has all been settled once and for all on that cruel – but utterly glorious – cross.

4. what are the advantages of becoming a Christian?

Many people will give you the impression that, if you become a disciple of Jesus Christ, life will become grey and dull, a round of churchgoing and curtailed enjoyment. Nothing could be further from the truth. Jesus said he came to give us life in all its fullness (John 10:10). The Gospels introduce us to a Jesus who was delightful company. People walked miles to be with him. And they were folk from widely different backgrounds, who normally would have had nothing in common. Judges and soldiers, fishermen and prostitutes, all found his company irresistible. He cheerfully broke the taboos which kept people apart in Judaism's highly structured society. He mixed with top people and street people with equal ease. He was as much at home in the tavern as he was in the temple. Whoever you are, you will find Jesus is the most wonderful companion you have ever had. And the Christian life is essentially companionship with him. All other friends may let you down, or even give you up. Not he. 'The Lord has promised that he will not leave us or desert us' (Hebrews 13:5). He is the risen Jesus, vibrantly alive. And here are some of the things he offers us if we put our lives in his hand.

He gives meaning to our lives. If we sprang from plankton and are heading for extinction, there can be no overall purpose or meaning in human life. That is why there is so much despair among modern artists, writers and film-makers. But, if we are the product of a living God, who plans to relate to us throughout eternity, then this life is a time of training and preparation for a wonderful goal after we die. And while we are alive, there is tremendous fulfilment in seeking to please God in all we do.

He gives enjoyment to our lives. Jesus promised to give his own joy and peace to his followers, and he does. So we can revel in our joys, knowing who is their ultimate source. We can appreciate beauty, truth, goodness, creativity, and the natural world all the more because we know they each display something of his handiwork and character. Our pains and sorrows are lit up by the assurance that God will not allow anything to befall us that ruins his ultimate purposes of good for our lives. And when times are tough, we can cheerfully accept them with some equanimity, seeing that they are designed to refine our lives and make them more Christlike.

He gives motivation to our lives. If there is no God, and I am on my own, there is nothing to restrain my innate selfishness apart from acquired habits – or the fear of discovery. I can be nice to others if it pays me. If not, I can be a perfect brute, so long as I can get away with it. But not if God is alive and well, and I am in touch with him! My delight will be to do his will and to reflect something of the generous, compassionate, wholesome character displayed so dazzlingly in Jesus Christ. 'I always do what pleases him [my Father],' said Jesus on one occasion (John 8:29). That attitude begins to rub off on us, too.

He gives power to our lives. Once we are in touch with God, we are not left to the best that our human resources are capable of. He offers to put a new moral strength into our lives so that we can begin to achieve the good things which had seemed so elusive, and progressively live more as we know we should. Once Jesus Christ is invited on board our lives, a new moral revolution begins. He not only makes character changes for the better, but he gives a new dynamic to live for others – and enjoy it!

He gives a new hope to our lives. Human beings cannot survive very long without hope. The trouble is that most of our hopes either disappoint or are very short term. But if God exists, and if Jesus rose triumphant from the grave, you can have complete confidence about the destiny of this world and

of yourself. The decisive battle has been won. The outcome is assured. But apart from God there is no long-term hope. Without him, every year that we live over the age of twenty is 'over the hill', as we head towards the unrelieved destiny of illness, death and extinction.

He gives new and profound relationships in our lives. Jesus does this in two ways. One is through a marvellous sense of belonging with fellow-believers wherever you go in the world. There is no society or club that can match this Christian fellowship, which we call the worldwide church. You may never have met the other Christians before, but the sense of being members of the same family, rescued by the same Lord, and lived in by the same Holy Spirit brings a depth of relationship that is unsurpassed.

The other way Christ changes our relationships is by giving us a bonding, an undying friendship with himself which no circumstance, no distance, no loneliness can remove. He promised he would be with his followers always, right up to the end of the world (Matthew 28:20) – and so he is. Any true believer will testify to the Lord's constant companionship, which is such a comfort and a strength. There is good reason for this. God has revealed himself in Scripture as the Trinity, three 'persons' in one God. That's where relationships, binding two or more people together in unity, have their source. He did not only invent relationships: he *is* relationship! He is three persons bound together as one. That is why our human loves and friendships are, at their best, the most satisfying things in life. Ask any lover. Alas, the relationship of two lovers sometimes fades in the course of time, but not the steadfast love of the Lord who will never abandon us.

5 rumours of life

If you have been with me this far in the book, I hope you have sensed that real Christianity is all about a relationship with the living God in the person of Jesus Christ himself. It is not primarily a matter of creeds or even church attendance. It is nothing less than a new life. Maybe the best analogy is when two people fall in love: they discover a new dimension to living. That is why I am so glad to include a number of 'real lives' in this book, people who have become fascinated by 'rumours of life' that they have heard, and have gone on to discover the overflowing life that Jesus offered to his disciples (John 10:10). I hope you have reached the point where you would like to test the reality of all this for yourself. But I imagine that, very wisely, you are asking a few questions first.

I. what will it cost?

There is a cost to everything in life that is worth having. And there is a serious cost to the Christian life. One shrewd

person put it like this: 'The entrance fee to the Christian life is nothing at all – but the annual subscription is all you have got.' The cost of our salvation was paid by Christ on the cross, and some people never become his disciples because they are too proud to accept that as a gift. But once you do start to follow Jesus you will find that there is a substantial cost.

It will cost you your sins. Jesus calls us to repent, or change direction. That means a fond farewell to all the stuff in our lives that we know is muck. It does not mean that you will never fall into muck again: we all do from time to time. But it does mean that you have deliberately changed direction. You cannot rid yourself of your failings: if you could, you would not need Jesus. Jesus can rid you of them over the years: but you have to let him. You cannot both have Christ as your Saviour and also hold on vigorously to the bad things in your life from which he wants to set you free.

It will cost you your selfishness. We are all pretty keen on our independence. We like to run our lives as we please. And when Jesus meets us, he comes as Lord and Master as well as Saviour and Friend. In a word, he's the boss: we are the learners. And that is not easy for us. But it makes sense, does it not? After all, he knows you inside out. He knows what is best for you and where you fit in with his good purposes. So why not put yourself without reserve into his hands? You will often have an argument with him over some issue, and will want to withdraw some of that initial surrender. But are you willing in principle to say, 'Lord, come and take over the whole of my life. I want to be yours for good and all'? That is what he longs for. And in that surrender, curiously enough, you will find a freedom you never dreamed of, for you are not handing yourself over to an institution or a rule book, but to someone who loves you dearly and will never harm you. He is utterly to be trusted. What does not work is a half-hearted Christian life. I've tried it, and it is sheer misery!

It will also cost you your secrecy. How we love to think that

our religion is our own affair and that it is something we don't talk about. Well, that is not an option for us if we start taking Jesus seriously. He warned that if we did not acknowledge him before our fellow men, he would not acknowledge us before his Father in heaven. He calls us to be candles in the surrounding darkness, salt among the rotting meat, a city set on a hill that cannot be hidden. Jesus always seems to have called people to open decision and discipleship. It is good for us, actually. It helps to nail our colours to the mast. Whoever heard of being a soldier and yet ashamed to wear the uniform? Don't think that if you start to follow Jesus you will be able to keep it quiet. After all, what use to him is a secret disciple? He wants people who will start to change society, and be unembarrassed to be known as his followers. So it is costly to come and follow him. Make no mistake about it. But it is more costly to say no to his call. Without Christ we will never know the joy of having past failures erased. We will never know the joy of reconciliation with the God who made us. We will miss the companionship of the worldwide Christian family. And we will miss out on heaven – miss what we were designed to enjoy.

Jesus constantly reminded his hearers that they would have to live with the consequences of their decision. In one of his famous parables he invites all and sundry to the banquet of the Christian life, but tells us in the same story that the door is shut on those who refuse the invitation. Does that seem a bit hard? Not at all. God makes complete provision for us to come into his presence, forgiven and cleaned up – and all at his expense. If we reject the means he has generously provided, how can we presume on his mercy? If we spit in his eye and spurn his love, we have only ourselves to blame for missing the party. We need to choose.

2. how could I be sure?

Just suppose you were to take this step of commitment to

Jesus Christ, how could you be sure that it would make any difference? Indeed, how could you be sure he will accept you?

These are vital questions, and it is important to face them before going any further. An ill-considered decision is no use to any of us. Fortunately, this is a matter which can be settled without too much difficulty – because it rests on the trustworthiness of a God who is utterly reliable.

Let's get one pseudo-problem out of the way first. Some people say, 'We cannot possibly know whether or not we are Christians: that would be arrogant. We aren't meant to be sure.' Assurance would certainly be arrogant if Christian discipleship were a matter of our own achievements. Who could possibly claim to be good enough? But the marvellous thing is that God offers us forgiveness, new life, membership of his family, as a gift. It is an act of supreme generosity on his part. We have to accept it as a gift, or we do not get it at all. How insulted you would be if you invited me to a marvellous dinner at great expense, and I said, 'I'll pay you 20p towards it.' And so when God invites us to his banquet, we can only say in wondering gratitude, 'I'm coming home. Thank you so much for such a generous invitation.' In a word, we are not relying on our achievements, but on God's solid, datable gift to us in the coming, dying and rising of Jesus of Nazareth. So there is no question of arrogance when Christians are sure that they belong. Would you adopt a child into your family and not mean that child to know that he or she belongs? Would you give someone a car and not mean them to know it is theirs? Of course not! Well, neither does God. 'By God's sheer undeserved generosity you have been saved. It is not due to your own achievements at all, but to God's free gift' (Ephesians 2:8–9, my translation). 'Very well,' you may say. 'I can see I am meant to be sure whether or not I am a Christian. But how come?'

First, God the Father gives us his word that he welcomes into his own family all who accept Jesus for themselves. Listen. 'Some people accepted him ... So he gave them the right to be

the children of God' (John 1:12). God does not break his promises. Have you received Jesus? Then you *are* in the family.

Second, let's get some clarity on this matter of evil, or 'sin' as Christians often call it. The New Testament uses three main words for it in the original Greek, which can be translated as 'shortcoming', 'offence' and 'rebellion'. We have come short of God's standards. We have broken his laws. We are rebels against his love. That inevitably puts us in the wrong with him. It makes us guilty. But when we entrust ourselves to Jesus, we are totally forgiven, and things begin to change. It takes a long time to grow like him, but the guilt thing is dealt with at once. On the cross Jesus paid our debts in full, though it cost him hell. He pressed the 'delete' key, and our sins were wiped away. But it is a favourite ploy of the Enemy to remind us of past failures and tell us what a disaster we are. 'What, you a Christian? Don't kid yourself. There, you have done it again.' That sort of attack is very dispiriting until we learn to face the Enemy with the objective fact of Christ's death. Tell him you know you are a disaster, but that 'Christ carried the burden of our sins. He was nailed to the cross' (1 Peter 2:24), and the job never needs to be repeated. Tell the Tempter to get lost. He will soon give up tempting you to doubt that you are a Christian. He has plenty of other ploys!

Third, the Holy Spirit has been given us, and God does not revoke his gifts. It is the Spirit's job to assure us we belong. 'God's Spirit makes us sure that we are his children. His Spirit lets us know that together with Christ we will be given what God has promised' (Romans 8:16–17).

This sounds good, but how does the Spirit make his presence felt? There are a number of ways, and the apostle John tells us about them in his first letter.

There's a new sense of pardon. A wonderful sense that we are clean. 'If you do sin, Jesus Christ always does the right thing, and he will speak to the Father for us. Christ is the sacrifice that takes away our sins' (1 John 2:1–2).

There's a new desire to please God. Previously I did not care whether I pleased him or not. But now I care very much; I don't want to hurt the one I love. That is an evidence of inner change. 'We truly love God only when we obey him as we should, and then we know that we belong to him. If we say we are his, we must follow the example of Christ' (1 John 2:5–6).

There's a new attitude to other people. 'Those who belong to the devil refuse to do right or to love each other.' Again, 'If we have all we need and see one of our own people in need, we must have pity on that person, or else we cannot say we love God' (1 John 3:10, 17).

There's a new appreciation of Christian companionship. 'Our love for each other proves that we have gone from death to life' (1 John 3:14). John is speaking of fellow Christians. They may have seemed a strange bunch previously, but once we have responded to Christ's call we begin to find ourselves actually wanting to be with them, to learn from them and to encourage one another. Birds of a feather flock together.

There's a new power over evil. 'People who stay united in their hearts with him won't keep on sinning.' How is this possible? Because 'God's Spirit is in you and is more powerful than the one that is in the world' (1 John 3:6 and 4:4). This is where the other side of God's handling of evil comes in. He broke the back of it and paid the penalty for it once for all on the cross. But he gradually releases us from the power of evil through his unseen revolutionary force – who is God, the Holy Spirit. For once we have said 'yes' to Christ, the Holy Spirit enters our lives and becomes a permanent resident. He is stronger than the forces of evil to which we are so prone. And he will give us that strength to overcome if we cry out to him for help, when temptation strikes.

There's a new joy and confidence. Needless to say, Christians have to go through periods of pain and sadness like everyone else. But there is an underlying joy even then. It comes from fellowship with the Lord and support from his people. The apostle alludes to it in the first few verses of his

letter: 'We are writing ... because this makes us truly happy' (I John 1:4).

There's a new experience of answered prayer. We probably prayed previously (most people do) but were never quite sure that the prayer had got through. But once we have got linked up with the Jesus who died and rose again, that 'sound barrier' of sin and alienation, which blocked us off from God and made us feel we were praying to ourselves, has been pierced. Prayer will gradually become companionship with God. We shall delight to share things with him, and the answers will begin to come. 'We are certain that God will hear our prayers when we ask for what pleases him. And if we know that God listens when we pray, we are sure that our prayers have already been answered' (1 John 5:14–15). We do not always get what we ask, of course. But we do have the assurance of being heard. God will answer as he sees fit.

John sums it up in a delightful way. He says in effect, 'If you believe a man when he gives you his word about something, how much more believe God? If you don't, you are calling him a liar. And this is God's solemn word: He has given us eternal life, and this life is in his Son. He who has the Son has life, and he who does not have the Son of God does not have life' (see 1 John 5:10–12). Whether or not you have spiritual life depends on whether or not you have responded to the invitation of Jesus to share your life with him. If you have him and he has you, then you *have* eternal life. Not *will have* when you die: you have it already. God guarantees it. For his eternal life is all wrapped up in Jesus. If you have Jesus, you already have begun to taste a life with God that will last for ever. Not surprisingly, therefore, John concludes, 'You have faith in the Son of God, and I have written to let you know that you have eternal life' (1 John 5:13).

3. how do I begin?

You do not need a degree in theology or ten years in church

to start the Christian life. To begin this relationship with the risen Jesus Christ is very profound but very simple.

First, *there is something to admit.* You have broken God's laws, you have come short of his standards. Indeed, you are a rebel against him: you have for many years been paddling your own canoe and leaving him out. Well, there has got to be a change of direction. The Bible's name for this is 'repentance'. It means an abrupt about-turn – back to the God we have disobeyed and hurt. It means a willingness for him to clean up our lives and take us in hand. It means, if you like, handing in our weapons and taking his outstretched hand.

Not easy! We are proud. We find it hard to admit we are in desperate need of rescue from the consequences and the grip of our own self-centredness. But that is where the new life with Christ begins. We have to admit we are in the wrong before he can put us right.

Second, *there is something to believe.* You do not need to believe a great deal in order to become a Christian. But you do need to trust in the central truths of the Christian gospel, namely that God himself in the person of Jesus came to this earth to find you (among others). He died on the cross to pay your debts and delete your guilt. He is alive to be your friend, your strength, and your joy. Those truths are spelled out in the Christian year. Christmas – he came for you. Good Friday – he died for you. Easter – he lives for you. Pentecost – he offers to indwell you by his Spirit. That is the heart of Christian belief.

Third, *there is something to consider.* That is the cost of following Jesus. As we have seen above, the entrance fee is free (he paid it). The annual subscription is everything you have. That may seem very formidable. But, after all, in marriage millions of people every year are only too happy to pay their annual subscription of joyful self-giving and trying to please their partners. That is the cost, and the delight, of becoming a Christian.

Fourth, *there is something to do.* And that is, to accept

Jesus into your very life, and to trust in his death on the cross for you.

There is a famous verse in the Bible that has helped millions of people to come to a living faith. It runs like this: 'Listen! I am standing and knocking at your door. If you hear my voice and open the door, I will come in and we will eat together' (Revelation 3:20). It is as if our lives were a house. Jesus says he is willing to come in and share it with us only if we will invite him in. A superb, clear analogy. But the marvellous thing is that this is no mere figure of speech. Because when we turn away from our sin and give our lives to Jesus as Lord, then he does indeed come into us by his Holy Spirit. This is what makes us Christians. We may (or may not) have been baptized, gone to church, and lived a decent life. But if we have not opened up our lives to Jesus and asked him to come in, then we are not yet Christians in the full sense of that word. 'People who don't have the Spirit of Christ in them don't belong to him' (Romans 8:9). So said the apostle Paul – and he should know! That is the decisive step in becoming a Christian.

When Jesus left this earth he promised his followers that he would send them his invisible presence, his Holy Spirit, who would never leave them (John 14:16). This is what happened on the first day of Pentecost, and the promise stands for all Christians.

It all begins to become real when we open up to the Spirit of Jesus and invite him into our lives. That is, after all, a *reasonable* thing to do: he has proved his love by dying for us. It is a simple thing to do: anyone can open a door and let a visitor in. It is a *necessary* thing do: you can't have a relationship with someone who is still outside the door. It is an *unrepeatable* thing to do: 'The Lord has promised that he will not leave us or desert us' (Hebrews 13:5). And it is an *urgent* thing to do: if you refuse him now you will find it much harder to respond to his call later on.

So why not do it now?

You might care to use some such prayer as this:

'Lord, I admit that I have broken your law and fallen far short of what you would want me to be. Thank you for coming to find me, for dying on the cross and absorbing my guilt. Thank you that you are alive and willing to come into my life and start changing it. Please come in right now, and never leave me. Take me on as one of your disciples.'

You can be sure of the Lord's response to that. Did he not say if *anyone* hears my voice? Did he not say I *will* come in? There is no 'maybe' about it. If you have asked him in, he has come in as he promised. Jesus does not break his word. Listen to his gracious promise: 'Everyone that the Father has given me will come to me, and I won't turn any of them away' (John 6:37).

It may be that you are not quite sure whether or not you have made that commitment. It may be there was some hazy pencilled contract you made in the past that you have almost forgotten. Very well, pray to him now and make sure!

real lives

Trudy Chappell of Grimsby left the best fish and chips in England to study English, Drama and Education in Exeter. She worked for a year for the Student Union and has been a parish assistant in a small church in Canterbury.

All I ever wanted was to be successful! I wanted (1) to pass my exams, (2) to earn an enviably large annual income, (3) drive a GTi something or other, (4) live in a

'Habitat' country cottage *avec* Dave, Rob, Kev or whoever it happened to be, and (5) sport a chique Glenys Barber 'Makepeace' (remember her?) bob haircut. Quite arrogantly, I didn't anticipate any major blips snarling up the way ahead, although I quickly acknowledged that my track record with men made (4) unlikely, and that (5) simply wasn't me.

While sipping a drink (spiked by my friends) at a party, I fell to wondering just why it was that people always preferred eating each other rather than the nibbles provided. I had encountered my first 'blip'. Was there more to life than this? Parties, money, sex, money, image? Soon I was awash with questions which led me to wonder where a God, if there was one, fitted into the picture. I went to church looking for answers, but left convinced that God was nowhere to be found. After a brief flirtation with New Age philosophies, I decided on a path of indifference. Making sense of life was a thankless task ... too much hard work and disappointment.

A month down the line at university, I was hit by a sudden renewed curiosity about God. Some friends in hall admitted to reading the Bible and chatted openly about God; they spoke as though they really knew him. Their values were upside down as far as I could see, trusting their God enough to live the way he wanted them to. I once heard them pray, and was moved to tears as they thanked God for his love and for 'sending Jesus'. There was much I didn't understand, especially about the new 'name in the frame'. I hadn't got a clue about Jesus and decided that it was all getting just a little bit too serious for me. I boycotted all things 'God-like' for the next couple of weeks; but that didn't solve anything.

I became more and more aware of how empty my life really was. As I was feeling the weight of eighteen years' worth of

dirty linen on my shoulders, my friends spoke of how we have hurt a holy God with the things we have done wrong. I'd been horrible to my Dad from the year dot, selfish and greedy, lied till the cows came home, and felt completely trapped in muck. When they explained how Jesus, the Son of God, willingly died on a cross with my dirty linen on his back so that I could be forgiven, know God for myself and be free to live this different life, I tried to climb out of the window and escape.

Yet the plot made sense ... Convinced now that it was true, I got down on my knees and sobbed. I talked to God and said I was sorry for everything and asked Jesus to be part of my life.

That was seven years ago and things have certainly changed. I don't care so much for my ambitions (1) to (5). There are more important things in life to consider ... Back now to Michael to explain more.

what next?

When we say 'yes' to Jesus Christ and invite him into our lives, it is as if we had just got married to the most marvellous person in the world. Or, to change the analogy, as if we had got adopted into a wonderful family. It would be an enormous change. And so it is when we become committed Christians. We find that we have made a great Enemy as well as a great Friend. The Enemy is the devil. You may not believe in him right now: no matter, you will soon discover his power. He is far from pleased that you have taken a stand for Jesus Christ. If he can't get you back, he will do his level best to make you fall.

The first assault will almost certainly be doubt. 'How could I be sure he has accepted me? What if I don't feel any different?' Take heart. Almost everyone has these early doubts.

They are quite normal. But it is most important to learn how to handle them.

the contract

If we rely on our feelings alone, we shall be in serious trouble. It is unlikely that we shall feel very aware of Christ when we have a high temperature or a splitting head. But facts are not altered by feelings – though our enjoyment of them is! And the facts are plain. On the cross, Christ dealt with all the bad stuff in our life and cried out triumphantly, 'Finished!' God the Father has acquitted us of all that guilty past: it will never be raised against us again. There is a marvellous passage on this subject in Romans 8:31–39. Look it up. It could well become one of your favourite Bible passages. A third fact is that Christ's Spirit has come into our lives if we have asked him in. You may find it helpful to re-read section 2 of this chapter, *How could I be sure?* (pages 77–81). At any rate, our position is as certain as that of a bride who has just been married and received her wedding certificate: or of a youngster of no fixed address who has just been adopted into the royal family and been given his adoption certificate. When tempted to doubt in the early days, trust the contract, not the feelings.

going public

As we have seen, it will not do to settle for secret discipleship. We need to let it be known, just as we would if we had got married or had been adopted. At home, our lives are likely to be the most eloquent testimony to the change. The family knows us too well to be impressed by words alone! However, we do need to 'honestly say, "Jesus is Lord"' as well as 'believe with all [our] heart' (see Romans 10:9–10). So try to find someone today and tell them of the step you have taken. Find someone sympathetic to begin with! And if you have not

yet been baptized, start thinking about that. Remember, for Christians it is the badge of belonging.

learning from God

When we set out on an unknown journey, it is wise to take a map. Mercifully God has provided us with an excellent map for our Christian lives. It tells us both how we can get to know him better, and how we should live. It is a detailed and descriptive map of how we can progress in our lives until finally we meet him face to face. It is a comprehensive guide, with promises to claim, examples to follow, warnings to heed, and prayers to use. Above all, it brings us face to face with the Lord himself. He inspired this book. He reveals not just his will but himself in its pages. There is a lovely saying of Martin Luther about the prime reason for Bible reading: 'as we come to the cradle to find the baby, so we come to the Scriptures to find the Christ'. Feed on this book and you will grow. Neglect it and you will remain a spiritual dwarf.

Practically speaking, it is good to read a small section every day, praying that God will make it come to life for you and, like a meal, strengthen you for the day's work. Look out for commands and promises and things to thank God for or say sorry about. Be particularly attentive to what it tells you about Jesus and about yourself. Then pray to God about what you have learned. Ask him to strengthen you so that you can change, and put into practice what he has taught you. There are various Bible reading systems, such as those published by the Scripture Union, the Bible Reading Fellowship, *etc.*, which you might find a real help.

speaking to God

God, amazingly, is not too busy to lend a listening ear to us. All through the Bible we are given invitations to cast our burdens on him and he undertakes to carry them. We are bidden

to ask and we will receive, to seek and we will find, to knock and it will be opened to us. A lovely bit in one of the psalms goes like this. God is seen as inviting us to meet with him: 'Come and worship me.' And the psalmist responds: 'I will come, LORD' (Psalm 27:8, GNB). It is wonderful that God should give to you and me this unrestricted access into his presence. He is never too busy for us. He is never fed up to see us. And the Enemy hates it. He knows full well that prayer is the source of spiritual power.

If the Queen offered you an audience, I bet you would be there, bright-eyed and bushy-tailed, thrilled to bits with the privilege. Well, the King of kings invites us to have an audience with him, and not once in a life-time but on a regular basis. We can talk to him at any time, on any subject. And if we persist in sharing our happiness, our requests, our thanksgivings, our confessions with him, we will grow. Moreover, we will see clear and unmistakable answers to our prayers.

meeting with God's family

It has been well said that the Christianity which does not begin with the individual does not begin; but the Christianity which ends with the individual ends. Following Jesus is a community business, not a solo trip from the alone to the Alone. To use one of the Bible's favourite images, we are adopted into God's family. We need – and are not at liberty to choose – our brothers and sisters.

Sometimes the New Testament sees us as branches in a great tree, or stones in a building, or soldiers in an army, or limbs in a body. These pictures are always plural: you see, we are called into a new community. This is very important, because it slays a couple of common misconceptions.

One is that I am the macho type who can soldier on by myself: I have my own ideas about God and I do not need anything from you, thanks. That attitude is profoundly un-Christian. We are not meant to be rugged individuals who

fondly imagine we are independent. God tells us we can't cope adequately as Christians on our own, and we are not meant to try. We need each other. To fancy that we do not is to give way to an arrogance which stinks in God's nostrils.

The other misconception is that Christianity is meant to be confined to a special little 'God slot' in our lives. Nothing could be further from the truth. It is all about the kingdom of God, the community which is trying to make God king in every aspect of daily life. He wants to bring into being an alternative society to the selfish rat race which marks most of the Western world. He wants to cultivate in us not independence but interdependence. He wants us to be a rainbow people, of all shades and backgrounds, who reflect his sunlight against a dark and rainy sky. He wants us to be a compassionate people in a hard world. He wants us to show that it is possible, and infinitely attractive, to live an upright, unselfish, generous life marked by love for God and neighbour. This is not something any of us can do on our own. We need each other.

experiencing change

How, we wonder, can Jesus make a real difference to our lives? The answer lies in the Holy Spirit. As we have seen, when Jesus died that was not the end of him. He rose to life again and when he went to rejoin his Father in heaven he sent his Holy Spirit to live inside believers. That Holy Spirit is within you now. He is the key to living a progressively overcoming life.

I know that such a claim borders on the fantastic. It is like supposing the spirit of Handel or Elvis could come and indwell your personality, enabling you to reflect something of their genius. Of course, that cannot happen. But when God Almighty offers to come and share his life with you, who is to say that is impossible? It is not impossible, as millions of Christians will tell you, because it has happened to them. If you have opened up your life, it has begun to happen to you.

That is the answer God gives to our ongoing failure to live up to his standards. He lives within us, and will empower us with his mighty strength, if we ask him when temptation is becoming hot. He will fight for us, in us, and with us. And make no mistake, it is a fight. It is by no means a walk-over. God does not overwhelm our free decisions day by day, by forcing us to be good. Actually, we are just as weak as before we entrusted our lives to him. The only difference is that the mighty Spirit of God is on board now. We can draw on his strength – if we so choose. We can turn to him and ask his help when temptation strikes: or we can battle along on our own and get defeated, just as we so often did. But let's be clear on this. The Holy Spirit is God's answer to the moral defeat which spoils our freedom.

going for broke

A question which will become more and more insistent as we go on in the Christian life is this. Who are we going to live for? What is to be our guiding star? Ambition? Power? Money? A comfortable life? Sometimes these are burning passions: sometimes we slide into them without realizing. But life is short, and we need to make up our minds on such a crucial issue.

I want to end this book with a challenge that we take seriously the extent of Jesus' sacrifice for us, and in return offer him the whole of our lives. A challenge to allow him to direct us into paths he knows to be best for us and for his kingdom. He has given us particular talents and endowments. Let us choose to employ them in some way that furthers his principles of love and service to others, as befits citizens of the kingdom of heaven. It has very little to do with the actual occupations and careers we busy ourselves with. It has almost everything to do with our attitude, and the way we conduct ourselves in daily life. Jesus calls us to put him first in every aspect of our lives. He is either Lord of all or not Lord

at all. This will have a radical effect on how we treat other people and situations.

While at Cambridge and at the height of his sporting success, C. T. Studd rode the crest of the social wave. Yet inwardly he saw the emptiness of his own existence, living only for games, popularity and pleasure. During a Christian Union mission he discovered that Jesus had died for him: he responded by giving his life to Christ. In due course he gave up his wealth and an international cricketing career, and went as a missionary to three continents – with incalculable consequences for good. He said, 'If Jesus Christ be God and died for me, no sacrifice can be too great for me to make for him.'

To look more closely at Christianity, and what it means to be a follower of Jesus, read* Men as Trees, Walking ... *– the first-century Gospel of Mark ...

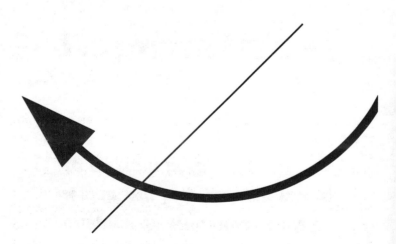

[postscript]